j363.728 Miller, Debra A.
MIL
        Garbage and
        recycling.

$32.45   Grades 7-9   05/05/2010

DATE			

Garbage and Recycling

by Debra A. Miller

LUCENT BOOKS
A part of Gale, Cengage Learning

GALE
CENGAGE Learning

Detroit • New York • San Francisco • New Haven, Conn • Waterville, Maine • London

LIBRARY OF CONGRESS CATALOGING-IN-PUBLICATION DATA

Miller, Debra A.
  Garbage and recycling / by Debra A. Miller.
      p. cm. -- (Hot topics)
  Includes bibliographical references and index.
  ISBN 978-1-4205-0147-6 (hardcover)
  1. Refuse and refuse disposal. 2. Recycling industry. I. Title.
  HD4482.M55 2009
  363.72'85--dc22
                                                            2009018371

Lucent Books
27500 Drake Rd.
Farmington Hills, MI 48331

ISBN-13: 978-1-4205-0147-6
ISBN-10: 1-4205-0147-X

Printed in the United States of America
1 2 3 4 5 6 7 13 12 11 10 09

Printed by Bang Printing, Brainerd, MN, 1st Ptg., 10/2009

CONTENTS

FOREWORD   **4**

INTRODUCTION   **6**
Our Hidden Garbage

CHAPTER 1   **11**
Garbage—Yesterday and Today

CHAPTER 2   **28**
The Recycling Solution

CHAPTER 3   **44**
Dealing with Hazardous Waste

CHAPTER 4   **60**
Waste Management—A Global Challenge

CHAPTER 5   **75**
New Waste Management Strategies for the Future

NOTES   **93**

DISCUSSION QUESTIONS   **98**

ORGANIZATIONS TO CONTACT   **100**

FOR MORE INFORMATION   **104**

INDEX   **107**

PICTURE CREDITS   **111**

ABOUT THE AUTHOR   **112**

FOREWORD

Young people today are bombarded with information. Aside from traditional sources such as newspapers, television, and the radio, they are inundated with a nearly continuous stream of data from electronic media. They send and receive e-mails and instant messages, read and write online "blogs," participate in chat rooms and forums, and surf the Web for hours. This trend is likely to continue. As Patricia Senn Breivik, the former dean of university libraries at Wayne State University in Detroit, has stated, "Information overload will only increase in the future. By 2020, for example, the available body of information is expected to double every 73 days! How will these students find the information they need in this coming tidal wave of information?"

Ironically, this overabundance of information can actually impede efforts to understand complex issues. Whether the topic is abortion, the death penalty, gay rights, or obesity, the deluge of fact and opinion that floods the print and electronic media is overwhelming. The news media report the results of polls and studies that contradict one another. Cable news shows, talk radio programs, and newspaper editorials promote narrow viewpoints and omit facts that challenge their own political biases. The World Wide Web is an electronic minefield where legitimate scholars compete with the postings of ordinary citizens who may or may not be well-informed or capable of reasoned argument. At times, strongly worded testimonials and opinion pieces both in print and electronic media are presented as factual accounts.

Conflicting quotes and statistics can confuse even the most diligent researchers. A good example of this is the question of whether or not the death penalty deters crime. For instance, one study found that murders decreased by nearly one-third when the death penalty was reinstated in New York in 1995. Death penalty supporters cite this finding to support their argument that the existence of the death penalty deters criminals from committing murder. However, another study found that states without the death penalty have murder rates below the national average. This study is cited by opponents of capital punishment, who reject the claim that the death penalty deters murder. Students need context and clear, informed discussion if they are to think critically and make informed decisions.

The Hot Topics series is designed to help young people wade through the glut of fact, opinion, and rhetoric so that they can think critically about controversial issues. Only by reading and thinking critically will they be able to formulate a viewpoint that is not simply the parroted views of others. Each volume of the series focuses on one of today's most pressing social issues and provides a balanced overview of the topic. Carefully crafted narrative, fully documented primary and secondary source quotes, informative sidebars, and study questions all provide excellent starting points for research and discussion. Full-color photographs and charts enhance all volumes in the series. With its many useful features, the Hot Topics series is a valuable resource for young people struggling to understand the pressing issues of the modern era.

INTRODUCTION

OUR HIDDEN GARBAGE

Garbage—also called trash, municipal waste, or refuse—is the by-product of our industrial age. It is also the result of an economic system that produces goods cheaply and encourages consumers to buy new products continually and consume foods in throwaway containers. We have truly become a disposable society; in America up to 80 percent of products are used once and then thrown away. In fact, according to the U.S. Environmental Protection Agency (EPA), the average American throws away 4.62 pounds (2kg) of garbage a day. Much of this discarded material is paper and plastic used for packaging. And the amount of garbage we produce has increased, despite widespread recycling efforts. In 2007, for example, Americans generated about 254 million tons (230 million metric tons) of municipal solid waste (MSW), and almost two-thirds of this waste was not recycled.

Older Dumps

Decades ago products were made to last longer, and people tended to repair rather than replace goods. Later nearly every city and town established an open-air, public dump, where citizens brought items that could not be otherwise reused, sold, or salvaged. As the population grew and people produced more garbage, city dumps grew as well, often turning into small mountains of smelly and increasingly toxic garbage.

New York City created the largest dump in the world—the Fresh Kills landfill located on Staten Island. (*Kill*, in this context, comes from a word of Dutch origin that means "creek" or "channel.") For more than fifty years, the dump served as the city's principal dumping site, receiving about 14,000 tons (12,700 metric tons) of garbage per day, eventually becoming an environmental wasteland. Eventually, it covered 2,200 acres (890ha) and stood over 200 feet (60m) high—so big that it can be seen from outer space. Fresh Kills was finally shut down in 2001 after accepting the remains of the World Trade Center following the terrorist attacks of September 11. Since then the state of New York has been working to clean up the area and make it a viable wetland that can once again support wildlife.

Hidden Landfills

Today in the developed world, most older open air dumps are gone, having been cleaned, covered up, or sometimes even turned into parks, housing developments, or commercial areas. And despite the fact that the total amount of garbage has grown substantially, most Americans and people in other developed countries no longer see what happens to their trash. Consequently, many no longer view garbage as a problem. Instead, each week residents fill their trash and recycling containers and watch state-of-the-art city trash trucks empty them and take the contents away. The system seems neat, clean, and orderly. However, the truth is that most of our garbage is still simply being buried in dumps, now called landfills—garbage sites that are well hidden from public view.

Compared to most older city dumps, modern landfills are gigantic, rising multiple levels and sometimes spreading over many thousands of square acres—some approaching the size of Fresh Kills. These new mega-landfills can take in thousands of tons of refuse per day, compared to older dumps, most of which could only handle dozens of tons daily. And the new landfills are no longer owned by cities; instead, these mega-landfills are operated by large, privately owned waste management companies that contract with cities to dispose of their trash. By processing much larger amounts of garbage in each mega-landfill, these companies can achieve economies of scale and reap lucrative profits.

Usually, the landfills are situated in poorer rural areas. Urban garbage is trucked hundreds of miles, often across state lines, before it reaches its final destination. For example, New York City, since the closure of its Fresh Kills dump, has sent its residential garbage to landfills in New Jersey, Ohio, Pennsylvania, South Carolina, and Virginia.

The Garbage Debate

Waste management officials and the U.S. Environmental Protection Agency say that these modern landfills, unlike the dumps of yesteryear, are built to protect human health and the environment. They are constructed in areas that are not prone to flooding or earthquakes, and they are designed to limit noxious water or air emissions that can cause groundwater contamination or air pollution.

The Fresh Kills landfill on Staten Island in New York City is the largest dump in the world. It received approximately 14,000 tons of garbage per day before being shut down in 2001.

Most landfills, for example, are lined to prevent dangerous by-products from seeping into surrounding soils and water tables. In many landfills, methane gas and other chemical compounds released as organic parts of the garbage degrade are captured and either destroyed by flaring or used as an energy source. Most modern landfills also do not accept many hazardous substances that once were routinely thrown into dumps.

Critics, however, see modern waste management systems as an inadequate solution to the garbage problem. Environmentalists argue that even the best landfill lining will someday deteriorate and allow toxins to escape into the environment. In addition, according to environmental critics, most of the methane produced by landfills is released into the atmosphere, contributing to global warming. Some critics of modern landfills want the entire system of modern garbage disposal to be changed. They charge that by hiding the garbage problem from public view, the current system leads to increasing amounts of garbage in order to boost profits for manufacturers and private waste management companies. They envision a comprehensive, sustainable waste system that limits or prohibits the production of disposable items and excessive packaging, requires product manufacturers to recycle their products, and mandates residential recycling and composting —in order to reduce the amount of waste in the first place.

The garbage situation in less-developed parts of the world is even more of a concern to environmentalists and health experts. Poorer countries often cannot afford trash collection systems or technologically advanced landfills, so mountains of trash build up on residential streets and in open-air dumps, raising health, safety, and environmental issues.

Some developing countries have even begun to import trash from richer nations, increasing their revenue but adding to their garbage woes. Some of this imported trash is so-called e-waste— discarded computers, cell phones, or other technology products —which contains highly toxic heavy metals and other harmful substances. Workers are hired to disassemble and recycle these items, typically with little or no safety or health precautions, exposing them and the environment to dangerous toxins and pollution.

Garbage disposal is therefore a truly global issue with no cheap or easy solutions. Proposals for addressing this age-old problem involve not only better disposal services and policies and the use of new technology, but also movements toward sustainability that could bring major changes in the way goods are manufactured, sold, and marketed around the world. New approaches to garbage disposal, most environmental experts agree, will be critical to how economies will function in coming decades and whether governments can or will protect humans and the earth itself.

GARBAGE—YESTERDAY AND TODAY

The amount of garbage generated by the modern world's human population is enormous and growing. And much of today's refuse contains nonbiodegradable plastics or toxic chemicals and metals that are difficult to separate from organic wastes. Environmentalists claim this human-waste stream is creating serious health and environmental problems that must be addressed. Some commentators, however, suggest that these claims are exaggerated and that there is still plenty of room to store the world's trash.

The History of Garbage

Historically, the human population generated very little trash. The number of people in the world at the beginning of human civilization was quite small compared to today, and their impact on natural resources was negligible. What little garbage was produced—mainly human and animal wastes and ash from wood fires—was fully biodegradable and had virtually no environmental impact. Later, as civilizations developed and populations lived in denser communities and cities, humans began to produce more wastes. Up until the twentieth century, however, most types of human garbage were reused and recycled. As historian Susan Strasser explains:

> Merchants continued to sell most food, hardware, and cleaning products in bulk. Their customers practiced habits of reuse that had prevailed in agricultural communities. . . . Women boiled food scraps into soup or fed them to domestic animals; chickens, especially, would eat almost anything and return the favor with eggs. Durable

items were passed on to people of other classes or generations, or stored in attics or basements for later use. Objects of no use to adults became playthings for children. Broken or worn-out things could be brought back to their makers, fixed by somebody handy, or taken to people who specialized in repairs.[1]

Materials that could not be repaired or reused were typically sold or given to junk dealers. In Great Britain, for example, junk dealers known as "rag and bone men" would travel through residential neighborhoods by horse and cart in search of rags, paper,

A "rag and bone" man makes his rounds in the East End of London in the 1960s. In Britain, rag and bone men would travel by horse and cart through residential neighborhoods in search of materials that they could sell to support themselves.

pieces of metal or wood, fireplace ash, bottles, and anything else that they could sell to support themselves. Similar junk dealers worked the streets in most cities in America, and these small entrepreneurs, in turn, sold the junk to manufacturers who recycled it into new products. As Strasser writes: "[Rags] were in high demand for papermaking. . . . Grease and gelatine could be extracted from bones; otherwise bones were made into knife handles, ground for fertilizer, or burned into charcoal for use in sugar refining. Bottles were generally refilled."[2]

It was not until the advent of the Industrial Revolution—the historical period beginning in the late 1700s when the economies of the United States and many nations in Europe shifted from manual labor and hand tools to machines and factory manufacturing—that human-produced garbage became a critical issue. The full effect of the Industrial Revolution, however, was not felt until around the turn of the twentieth century, when systems of mass production and mass distribution were developed. This economic change produced many more products for people to purchase, and it also created jobs that helped to increase wealth that could be used to purchase products. As people were able to buy more and more new things, they stopped seeing value in broken and used items and began seeing these old items as trash. New forms of colorful advertising and packaging encouraged this burgeoning consumer culture.

At the same time, as companies grew in size, manufacturers stopped buying recycled goods from junk dealers, instead turning to other sources for raw materials or developing other production strategies. Papermakers, for example, began making paper from wood pulp instead of rags. Junk dealers could no longer sell bone scraps because large meat-packing companies now produced vast amounts of bones and other animal wastes for fertilizers and other products. And mechanization destroyed the recycling and refilling of bottles by allowing glass bottles to be made more quickly and cheaply.

All of these post-industrial trends contributed to a societal rejection of thrift and recycling, which in turn led to a growing pile of garbage. The once-closed and sustainable system of reuse and recycling was replaced with a one-way, open-ended system in which manufacturers create products from materials and energy extracted from the earth and sell those items to consumers, who in turn use them once or maybe a few times and then discard them as trash. Mass production and advertising techniques were perfected throughout the 1900s, creating today's all-encompassing consumer and convenience-oriented culture and economy. Journalist and filmmaker Heather Rogers describes this process:

> The streamlining of industrial production led to low-cost, ready-made goods. This culminated in the super-efficient post–World War II mass production line, which turned out everything from furniture and cars to blenders and sunglasses cheaply and at lightning speed. The corollary to the ensuing mass consumption was (and remains) mass wasting. Today, manufactured goods have become so inexpensive that it makes economic sense to throw things away rather than repair them; and this translates into massive piles of rubbish. . . . In short, our economic system relies, at its very core, on ever-greater piles of trash.[3]

A Mountain of Trash

In the United States alone, the amount of municipal waste tripled between 1960 and 2002. It reached a peak of 369 million tons (335 million metric tons) in 2002. Experts say the increase was due partly to population growth, but mostly to the consumption and disposal practices of average American residents. According to a 2003 report by the Earth Engineering Center of Columbia University, each and every American generates approximately 1.21 tons (1.1 metric tons) of garbage each year.

In 2007, the last year for which there are data, the EPA calculated that Americans produced 254.1 million tons (230.5 million metric tons) of municipal solid waste (MSW). Between 55 and 65 percent of this MSW came from residential sources. The rest—between 35 and 45 percent—was produced by commercial and institutional locations such as schools, hospitals, and businesses. According to the EPA, containers and packaging made up the largest portion of MSW (31 percent), followed by nondurable goods (products that are consumed or used quickly, such as toilet paper—24.5 percent), durable goods (products that are made

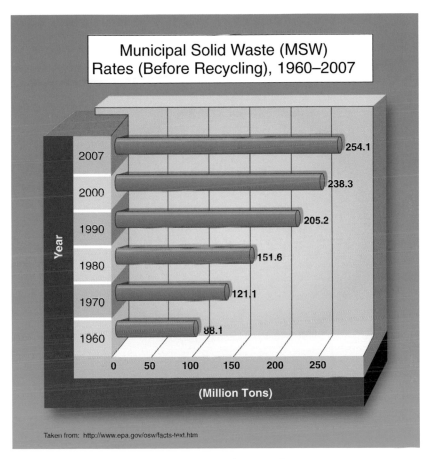

Municipal Solid Waste (MSW) Rates (Before Recycling), 1960–2007

Taken from: http://www.epa.gov/osw/facts-text.htm

to last more than three years, such as refrigerators—17.9 percent), yard trimmings (12.8 percent), and food scraps (12.5 percent). Paper and plastics led the list of materials discarded, at 32.7 percent and 12.7 percent respectively.

Of the 254.1 million tons (230.5 million metric tons) of waste, about 24.7 percent was recycled, about 8.6 percent was composted, and about another 12.6 percent was incinerated. A little more than half of the waste generated by Americans in 2007—about 53.9 percent (137 million tons or 124 million metric tons)—was buried in landfills. The EPA boasts that this percentage has decreased since 1980, when 89 percent of MSW was placed into landfills. Yet because the total quantity of garbage has increased over this period, the amount of waste landfilled in 2007 was still more than the amount buried in 1980.

Statistics about the amount of garbage produced globally are not easily found, but other developed countries such as Canada and the United Kingdom have waste management records similar to that of the United States. Some developed countries such as Japan, Denmark, and Germany appear to do a much better job at recycling the municipal-waste stream than the United States, while many less-developed nations have a growing trash problem. Overall, the amount of trash produced by earth's human population is increasing faster than the rate of population growth.

Dealing with Trash

In the 1900s growing amounts of trash required many industrialized societies to begin developing waste disposal systems. At first, cities simply hired workers to rake up trash from the streets on a regular basis and dump it anywhere they found convenient—in

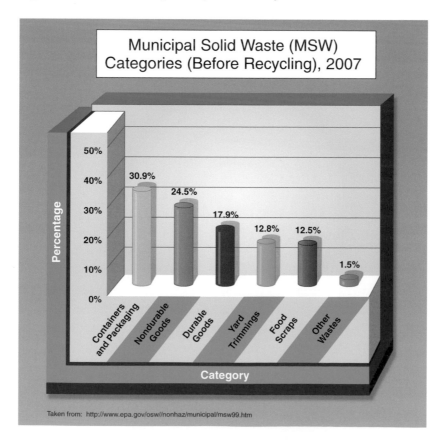

Taken from: http://www.epa.gov/osw//nonhaz/municipal/msw99.htm

rural areas, in wetlands, or in the ocean. Pig farms were also commonly used to dispose of cooked and uncooked food wastes, and people often burned the balance of their trash in their backyards.

The first public incinerators were built in the late 1800s in Great Britain and the United States, and in the next twenty years more of these were built. Many cities also established open-air dumps, where refuse was piled and sometimes burned. The incineration of garbage, however, produced prodigious amounts of smoke and soot, and the rotting garbage in open-air dumps smelled and attracted rats and other vermin. By 1945 many cities in the United States had replaced these open-air dumps and incinerators with more sanitary landfills, in which layers of garbage were covered with soil to prevent odors and avoid the ash and air pollution problems caused by burning. Small, private companies often performed the job of collecting and disposing of municipal garbage.

During this period, the U.S. government also began to regulate the disposal of municipal garbage. In 1934 the U.S Supreme Court banned dumping garbage into the ocean. Beginning in the 1950s the United States passed a series of clean air acts, beginning with the Air Pollution Control Act of 1955, which prohibited the open burning of garbage and sought to improve the quality of air in American cities. In 1965 Congress passed the Solid Waste Disposal Act to promote better management of solid wastes. The act authorized the U.S. Public Health Service to regulate solid waste disposal and recycling, provided financial assistance to states, and funded research on better methods of waste disposal. In 1970 President Richard Nixon created the Environmental Protection Agency (EPA), which thereafter became the central federal agency regulating issues relating to waste management.

The 1970s and 1980s brought more federal regulation of waste disposal. The Resource Recovery Act of 1970 sought to encourage recycling and energy recovery from wastes and authorized an investigation into the disposal of hazardous wastes. A few years later Congress passed the Resource Conservation and Recovery Act of 1976, which imposed various requirements on hazardous waste disposal. Additional restrictions were imposed by the Hazardous and Solid Waste Amendments of 1984. Many existing landfills could not meet these new safety regulations, and by the end of the 1980s almost two-thirds of the nation's landfills had shut down. This led to a renaissance in recycling, as many cities and localities instituted curbside recycling programs to try to limit the amount of garbage that had to be discarded.

EVERY AMERICAN CITY

"Every American city, up until about the middle of the twentieth century, dumped its rejects on nearby scraps of low-value land."—Elizabeth Royte, science and nature writer.

Elizabeth Royte, *Garbage Land: On the Secret Trail of Trash.* New York: Little, Brown, 2005, p. 50.

Various other environmental controls were put in place in the 1990s that again impacted the U.S. waste management system. In October 1991, for example, the EPA established regulations for municipal solid waste landfills that required a bottom liner and a system to collect and treat leachate—liquid wastes that seep through landfills—to protect groundwater. New EPA rules also imposed restrictions on landfill locations, preventing them from being placed near airports (to reduce the risk of planes colliding with birds that are attracted to landfill areas), in wetlands, in floodplains, or on earthquake faults, and set minimum landfill design and operation standards that included monitoring of groundwater to prevent contamination. These new controls dramatically changed the way garbage is processed in America. Most small waste management companies could not afford to operate under the new mandates, but bigger operators saw them as an opportunity to compete for the trash business of many cities and municipalities.

This consolidation process produced a system of waste management in which the majority of the nation's trash business belongs to several large corporations. In fact, just three companies—Waste Management, Allied Waste, and Republic Services—collect more than half the nation's trash at various locations around the country. And instead of using a number of smaller landfills located close to garbage sources, these large cor-

In order to help regulate the disposal of municipal garbage, President Richard M. Nixon created the Environmental Protection Agency (EPA) in 1970, which became the central federal agency regulating issues relating to waste management.

porations developed a system of trucking trash long distances to mega-landfills where they could achieve greater economies of scale and make larger profits. Not surprisingly, the number of active landfill sites in the United States has shrunk considerably. According to the Web site Blue Egg, "In 1988, there were nearly 8,000 landfills across the country; in 1999, there were 2,314; and by 2005, there were only 1,654."[4]

Effects of Garbage on the Environment and Human Health

Despite the actions taken by the federal government and the EPA to regulate garbage disposal, environmental experts remain concerned about the continuing effects of garbage on human health and the environment. Although many old-style municipal dumps have been cleaned up since the days of open-air, unregulated garbage dumping, health advocates say that thousands of these sites were simply abandoned. Some of these lands have since

Leachate at the Lycoming County landfill in Montgomery, Pennsylvania, is shown being treated in 2006. Leachate is a toxic brew of petroleum-based chemicals mixed with water.

been converted to new uses without cleaning up what lies underground. According to the advocacy group Zero Waste America, "It is not unusual to find old landfills or randomly buried hazardous and non-hazardous waste under new or old homes, on farmland, or on commercial property—in cities, suburbs, and rural areas."[5] These sites may still be leaking toxins into groundwater and air, or otherwise polluting the environment, including the farms, homes, offices, or stores that may now be perched on top of them. The only way to tell for sure that a site is safe is to conduct environmental testing of the soil and air.

TRASH IS NOT AN ISSUE

"All the American waste of the entire twenty-first century will fit into a single landfill."—Bjorn Lomborg, a Danish author, academic, and environmental writer.

Bjorn Lomborg, *The Skeptical Environmentalist: Measuring the Real State of the World.* New York: Cambridge University Press, 2001, p. 208.

Older dumps and landfills are known to produce various forms of pollution. As the environmental group Natural Resources Defense Council (NRDC) noted in a 1997 report,

"Among . . . the nation's most hazardous and contaminated locations, more than 20 percent are former municipal landfills."[6] As organic wastes decompose, they release poisonous gases such as carbon dioxide and methane into the atmosphere. If methane makes its way into people's basements, it can cause explosions. In addition, the decaying organic wastes create liquid that collects toxins as it seeps through dumps and landfills. Experts say this liquid—known as leachate—is typically a toxic brew of petroleum-based chemicals mixed with water.

Toxic Stew

Over 210 chemicals commonly used in household and consumer products or produced by industrial processes typically end up in residential garbage sites. Perhaps surprisingly, household products such as cleaning agents and pesticides are the source of many highly dangerous chemicals. Another human-made chemical abundant in landfills is phthalate, a substance known to interfere with human hormone functions; phthalate is commonly found in plastic wrap, soft plastic toys, plastic medical equipment, and household products.

ANCIENT DUMPS STILL POLLUTING

"The dumps of the Roman empire, more than 2,000 years old, are still leaching heavy metals today."—Blue Egg, an e-media company that promotes sustainable living.

Blue Egg, "Landfills: Waste Is a Terrible Thing to Mind." www.blueegg.com/article/Land fills-Waste-Is-a-Terrible-Thing-to-Mind.html.

Other common industrial chemicals in municipal garbage include numerous agricultural pesticides, as well as industrial solvents. Two solvents—trichloroethylene, a human-made chlorinated solvent widely used in industry to remove grease from metal parts and textiles, and perchloroethylene, a chemical mainly used as a dry-cleaning agent—are of great concern because they are considered to be carcinogenic (cancer causing) to humans. Adding to this

Dan Jacobson, of Environment California, points to a pair of baby items containing chemicals that some scientists say are hazardous to children. Phthalate is a man-made chemical that is abundant in landfills and is commonly found in soft plastic toys.

toxic soup may be dangerous heavy metals such as lead from old paint, mercury from alkaline batteries, or cadmium contained in e-waste such as old cell phones and computer monitors. These heavy metals are extremely poisonous to animals and humans.

As these toxins are released into surrounding air, groundwater, and soils, they can pollute the environment and potentially harm human health. In fact, various studies have shown that there are health risks for people who live near landfills, including increased rates of certain types of cancer. For example, a 1989 study by the EPA that examined 593 waste sites in 339 U.S. counties found elevated cancers of the bladder, lung, stomach, and rectum in counties with the highest concentration of waste sites. In addition, a study published in 1998 by researchers from the London School of Hygiene and Tropical Medicine reported a greater risk of birth defects in babies born to mothers who live close to landfills—specifically an elevated risk of neural-tube defects (spina bifida and anencephaly), malformations of the cardiac septa (a hole in the heart), and malformations of the arteries and veins. Another study by the Institute for Health and the Environment at the State University of New York at Albany, published in 2006, found that people living near a landfill may develop reduced immune function that can lead to an increased risk of infections. The study found, for example, that children living near

The *Mobro* Garbage Barge Odyssey

In 1987 the *Mobro* garbage barge—a ship carrying nearly 3,200 tons (2,900 metric tons) of trash from the city of Islip, New York—became the symbol of the growing problem of garbage disposal as it traveled on a 6,000-mile (9,656km), six-month odyssey looking for a place to dump its cargo. The *Mobro* began its journey on March 22, 1987, headed for Morehead City, North Carolina, which had agreed to accept the ship's load of refuse. State officials in North Carolina, however, decided not to accept the *Mobro's* cargo, and the barge next set off for Louisiana, home of the *Mobro's* captain. After Louisiana refused to accept the load of garbage, the *Mobro* tried the countries of Mexico, Belize, and the Bahamas, each of which also refused to take the New York trash. The *Mobro* eventually returned to New York, where officials in Brooklyn finally decided to incinerate its cargo of garbage. Commentators agree that the *Mobro* helped to raise the public's awareness about the issue of garbage disposal and the need for recycling.

waste sites are hospitalized more frequently with acute respiratory infections and asthma.

Air Pollutants

Yet another type of pollutant produced by landfills—landfill gas—contributes significantly to global warming, according to most experts. Landfill gas is composed of two greenhouse gases responsible for global warming—methane and carbon dioxide. In fact, as the environmental group Environmental Defense Fund (EDF) explains, "Methane, the main gas in landfill emissions, is 25 times more potent in terms of warming potential than CO_2 [carbon dioxide] and it's released from landfills across the country as a natural byproduct as waste decomposes."[7] And according to the EDF, "Municipal solid waste landfills are the second largest source of human-related methane emissions in the United States, accounting for nearly 23 percent of emissions in 2006."[8]

Food Wastes

A large part of the American waste stream is made up of food wastes. In fact, according to some estimates, more than 40 percent of all food produced in America is not eaten but simply thrown away. Experts say wasting food in this way harms the environment. First, enormous amounts of fossil fuel are used to produce, transport, and store food products, and throwing away good food both squanders these resources and unnecessarily produces carbon emissions, which cause global warming. The disposal of leftover food in landfills further contributes to climate change because rotting organic matter releases methane, another potent greenhouse gas. Food waste also costs money—according to some estimates, about $600 per household each year. To address this problem, the U.S. Environmental Protection Agency (EPA) recommends buying less food by planning dinners, using shopping lists, and ordering sensibly at restaurants. Unsold food or unpicked crops can also be used to feed the poor or added to food for livestock. If food wastes cannot be consumed, the EPA recommends composting them in order to keep the wastes out of landfills and create natural fertilizer that can be used on plants and gardens.

Incinerators also pose health risks. As the NRDC explains, "Municipal waste incinerators—like landfills—generate a wide range of toxic air pollutants—including dioxins, furans, heavy metals such as mercury, cadmium, and lead, acid gases, and fine particles —as well as contaminated ash."[9] For this reason, incineration plants are subject to many regulatory and legal requirements. The burdens of regulation, as well as vocal opposition from citizens living near proposed incineration sites, have made incineration a disfavored method of trash disposal in the United States.

Modern Landfills

Waste management companies and some commentators, however, maintain that the threat to health and the environment from modern landfills is negligible. The goal of modern landfills, they point out, is to create a dry tomb that cannot be permeated by water, in order to mummify the garbage and sequester it in the earth. And in modern landfills, methane gas is typically collected, piped to the top of the landfill, and then either flared—that is, burned off—or used as fuel to create energy. This system, industry experts argue, prevents most of the pollution once caused by dumping and decreases the amounts of carbon and methane that otherwise could be released into the atmosphere. As the National Solid Wastes Management Association explains, "The engineered systems in a modern landfill ensure protection of human health and the environment by containing leachate that can contaminate groundwater, preventing the infiltration of precipitation that generates leachate after closure of the landfill, and collecting landfill gas that can be used as an energy source or destroyed."[10]

New Landfills Are Safe

"Today's landfill siting and design features essentially eliminate the potential for problems posed by older landfills—a fact confirmed by the EPA."—Daniel K. Benjamin, economics professor and former adviser to President Ronald Reagan.

Daniel K. Benjamin, "Eight Great Myths of Recycling," Property and Environment Research Center, September 2003, p. 9. www.perc.org/pdf/ps28.pdf.

And the country's waste managers maintain that there is still plenty of space in existing landfills to handle future garbage. According to James Thompson with Chartwell Information, a company that collects information about waste disposal, the United States currently has sufficient landfill capacity to last another eighteen years. And when that capacity is gone, Thompson notes, more landfills can be licensed and built. Professor Daniel Benjamin agrees, arguing, "Even though the United States is larger,

A plastic covering is shown at the Fresh Kills landfill in New York. Many environmental advocates do not believe that modern landfills are safe because these liners may eventually crack or leak.

more affluent, and producing more garbage, it now has more landfill capacity than ever before."[11]

Despite these assurances, environmental advocates are not convinced that modern landfills are safe. Modern landfills contain many of the same toxic materials found in older dumps, they say, and their liners have a limited lifetime. In fact, some estimates say liners may crack or leak after just a few decades. The state-of-the-art landfill linings now mandated by the EPA, for example, are typically made of a plastic material called HDPE and are only about 0.1 mm (.04 inches) thick. Certain common materials, such as bleach and vinegar, can cause these linings to become brittle and degraded. Indeed, even the EPA admits that all liners eventually deteriorate and leak, stating:

> Eventually synthetic liners will degrade and leachate collection systems will cease operation. . . . No liner can be expected to remain impervious forever. As a result of interactions with waste, environmental effects, installation problems, and operating practices, liners eventually may degrade, tear, or crack and allow liquids to migrate out of the unit. . . . These technologies (double liners and leachate collection systems) may not effectively reduce the longer-term risk for landfills, especially for persistent and mobile compounds, because the containment system may only delay leachate release from the landfill until after post-closure, when the cap and leachate collection system begin to fail.[12]

As a result of these concerns about landfill safety, cities across the United States have sought, whenever possible, at least to reduce the amount of garbage that is placed into landfills by separately processing hazardous products, composting organic wastes, and recycling various materials.

CHAPTER 2

THE RECYCLING SOLUTION

Once a common way to dispose of trash, recycling today is experiencing a renaissance. Recent increases in the amounts of garbage, combined with heightened environmental awareness in developed countries such as the United States, have led to numerous government programs for recycling wastes. Most of these programs are voluntary, although some cities have recently begun to mandate recycling. Overall, recycling is widely viewed as beneficial to the environment and human health, although some commentators view it as a flawed solution to the garbage problem.

The Birth of Modern Recycling Programs

Even though recycling was commonly practiced by all households during pre-industrial ages, large-scale recycling programs did not arise until the twentieth century. The first organized programs were created in the 1930s and 1940s, when a worldwide depression limited people's ability to purchase new goods and the outbreak of World War II dramatically increased demands for certain materials. Throughout the war, goods such as nylon, rubber, and various metals were recycled and reused to produce weapons and other materials needed to support the war effort. After the war ended in 1945, however, the United States and other countries experienced a postwar economic boom that produced many new products and caused recycling to fade into oblivion for several decades.

It was not until the environmental movement of the 1960s and 1970s that recycling once again emerged as a popular idea. This movement began in 1962 with the publication of Rachel Carson's book *Silent Spring*, detailing the toxic effects of the chemical DDT on birds and their habitats. The book raised the consciousness of many people, both in the United States and abroad, about the dangers to the environment from chemicals and other toxins produced by modern industries. In the United States, the hippie culture in particular embraced the cause of environmentalism and agitated for various environmental changes, including the increased recycling of wastes. In 1970 environmental activists organized the first Earth Day to bring national attention to environmental issues, including the problem of increasing wastes and the need for recycling.

That same year the United States created the U.S. Environmental Protection Agency (EPA), which soon began to regulate garbage disposal to ensure public health and environmental safety. The closing of many municipal landfills in the wake of these new EPA regulations, in turn, led to a shortfall of landfill space in the 1980s. This problem was highlighted by the odyssey of the *Mobro* garbage barge—a boat filled with trash that departed New York in 1987 and traveled down the North and South American coasts for months looking for a place to offload its cargo. This incident helped raise the consciousness of Americans about the need for recycling, and slowly, recycling caught on as the most environmentally friendly way to reduce the expanding stream of human garbage and the pollution it causes.

There was a shortage of landfill space in the 1980s, which caused the Mobro *garbage barge to travel down the coast of North and South America for 155 days looking for a place to dump its 3,000 tons of waste.*

The Growth of Recycling

Due to Americans' growing acceptance of recycling, over the last several decades the amount of waste recycled has increased each year in the United States. One by one, cities and municipalities have voluntarily implemented convenient curbside recycling programs, and laws have required the use of recycled content in certain manufacturing processes. One of the first curbside collection programs was established in 1973 in California. It collected mostly newspapers and other kinds of paper, but as the size of the waste stream grew and the costs of landfilling increased, other states and localities gradually adopted similar programs, and many expanded the types of recyclables these programs collected. Today recycling is ubiquitous across the United States. According to an article written by garbage experts Heather Rogers and Christian Parenti in 2002, "More Americans recycle than vote."[13] The latest EPA statistics (2005) show the

A child's toy and plastic packaging are recycled at the San Francisco Recycling Center in 2008. The city of San Francisco is the leader in recycling across the United States and accepts a huge range of items, including many plastics.

United States has 8,550 curbside recycling programs. And many municipalities that have not yet established curbside recycling have at least created drop-off recycling programs, adding to the amount of wastes that are kept out of landfills. Many cities also have added municipal programs to collect organic wastes such as yard trimmings.

RECYCLING A GREAT SOLUTION

"Recycling saves energy, preserves natural resources, reduces greenhouse-gas emissions, and keeps toxins from leaking out of landfills."—Marc Gunther, a writer and speaker on business and the environment.

Marc Gunther, "The End of Garbage," *Fortune*, March 14, 2007. http://money.cnn.com/magazines/fortune/fortune_archive/2007/03/19/8402369/index.htm.

In 2007, for example, the EPA reported that the nation recycled and composted 85 million tons (77 million metric tons), or 33.4 percent of all municipal solid wastes—a vast increase from 1960, when only 6.4 percent was recycled. And this rise in recycling has occurred despite the fact that the total amount of waste has increased, from 3.7 to 4.6 pounds (1.7 to 2.1 kg) per person per day between 1960 and 2007. In fact, as the NRDC notes, "The amount of material we recycle today . . . equals the total quantity of garbage the United States produced in 1960."[14] Recycling success stories in 2007 included the recycling of 54 percent of paper and paperboard wastes and 64 percent of yard trimmings. And about 35 percent of metals such as aluminum, steel, and mixed metals were recycled—an effort that eliminated greenhouse gas emissions equivalent to taking 4.5 million cars from the road for one year.

Some American cities have far exceeded this national average, with cities in the West leading the way. Seattle, for example, implemented a mandatory recycling program in 2006 that requires households and apartments to keep all basic recyclables—paper, cardboard, glass, plastic, tin, aluminum, and yard clippings—out of ordinary garbage containers. Businesses must recycle paper, cardboard, and yard waste. Proponents of recycling view the program as a great success: In 2007 Seattle recycled 44 percent of its garbage, compared to the national average of 33.4 percent. The city hopes to increase its recycling percentage to 72 percent by 2025 and is preparing to make recycling of food scraps mandatory in 2009.

San Francisco, however, is the undisputed American leader in recycling. Even with a voluntary system, the city currently recycles 70 percent of its trash. The program's success is attributed to the fact that it accepts a wide range of items for recycling—including not only the usual items such as glass, paper, and aluminum cans, but also food scraps and a broad range of plastics. As city official Deanna Simon notes: "Pretty much anything plastic, except for plastic bags and Styrofoam, can now go into the recycling. . . . That includes a big wheel or a rubber ducky or a cup."[15] The city also runs an efficient program to recycle construction and demolition debris and other industrial materials such as sludge. San Francisco's mayor Gavin Newsom now wants to adopt a mandatory program for both recycling and composting. He aims to reach a goal of 75 percent recycling by 2010 and zero waste by 2020.

Recycling Basics

The three R's of conservation, as the EPA Web site notes, are "reduce/reuse/recycle"—that is, reduce the amount of trash thrown away in the first place, reuse containers and products whenever possible, and recycle or compost everything that can be recycled. The government's recycling plan also urges consumers to buy products made from recycled materials.

A long list of items can be easily recycled in most curbside programs, including all kinds of paper and cardboard, glass of all colors and types, plastic bottles, aluminum cans, and yard trimmings. In addition, a number of localities offer drop-off programs for recycling other items, such as household hazardous wastes (paints, cleaners, oils, batteries, and pesticides), automobile items (tires, used engine oil, car batteries, antifreeze), wood construction materials, certain metals, appliances, and consumer electronics. Only a few cities are experimenting with collection of food wastes for composting. Homeowners, however, can easily compost food wastes themselves by learning how to create a compost pile on their property where wastes can be turned into a nutritious material (called "compost") that can be used to fertilize gardens and other plants.

Most municipal recycling programs, however, only accept a few types of plastics. Determining which plastic items can be recycled can be ascertained by reference to a system of identification codes developed by the Society of Plastics Industries in 1988. These codes are

Cans and buckets of household hazardous waste are collected for safe disposal and recycling. Many cities offer drop-off programs for recycling these types of items.

stamped onto most household plastic items inside a triangle of arrows—a commonly used symbol for recycling in the United States. The number codes for plastics are as follows:

1. PET or PETE (polyethylene terephthalate—i.e., soda bottles)
2. HDPE (high-density polyethylene—i.e., milk jugs and water bottles)
3. Vinyl
4. LDPE (low-density polyethylene)
5. PP (polypropylene—i.e., long underwear)
6. PS (polystyrene—i.e., packaging "peanuts")
7. Other

According to estimates by the American Plastics Council, more than one-half of all U.S. communities now collect plastics for recycling, either at the curb or through drop-off centers. Yet the vast majority of these communities collect only PET and HDPE plastics (codes 1 and 2)—primarily milk and soda bottles. Most other plastic items, even if they are stamped with recycling symbols, go directly into landfills.

Recycling Benefits

The government and various environmental organizations regularly tout the many benefits of recycling. First and foremost, recycling reduces the amount of wastes that must be placed into landfills or incinerated. According to some experts, this saves money compared to the costs of other methods of trash disposal. As the National Recycling Coalition states, "Well-run recycling programs cost less to operate than waste collection, landfilling, and incineration."[16] Recycling advocates also argue that recycling programs create American jobs—not only jobs collecting recyclables, but also jobs in the industries that purchase and process the recycled materials and manufacture them into new products.

The most important benefits of recycling, however, relate to the environment and human health. Environmentalists say that by diverting materials from the waste stream going into landfills or to incinerators, recycling reduces air, ground, and water pollution that otherwise could result from these wastes. And the recycling of metals, glass, and other materials reduces pollution that would be

Reducing Wastes

Although recycling helps to keep some wastes out of landfills, recycling advocates say reducing the amount of waste created in the first place is even more effective. Individuals can have a direct effect on the waste stream by decreasing their consumption and taking several common sense steps. Since product packaging makes up most of the wastes generated in America, one of the best steps consumers can take is to avoid purchasing products that come with a lot of packaging. When shopping for groceries, for example, consumers can concentrate on buying bulk items and fresh fruits and vegetables rather than processed foods that often are heavily packaged. And when comparing products, consumers should consider whether the packaging can be recycled after the purchase and whether higher-quality products might last longer than cheaper items. Another good idea is to avoid both plastic and paper bags when shopping by substituting reusable shopping bags. Taking your own refillable beverage container to work, to the gym, or to coffee shops is a similar way to cut down on plastic water bottle and disposable cup wastes. All of these actions can add up to decrease wastes.

caused by the manufacturing of products from virgin materials. Using recycled materials also saves energy, advocates argue, because it takes less energy to use recyclables than to make a product from raw materials. As the National Recycling Coalition explains: "It takes 95% less energy to recycle aluminum than it does to make it from raw materials. Making recycled steel saves 60%, recycled newspaper 40%, recycled plastics 70%, and recycled glass 40%."[17] In addition, recycling reduces greenhouse gas emissions that contribute to global warming, because fewer goods are manufactured, fewer materials are producing methane in landfills, and fewer carbon-absorbing trees are cut down. In general, according to the EPA and many other sources, recycling reduces the stress on the environment, preserves natural resources, and helps sustain the environment for future generations.

The Limits of Recycling

Despite the benefits of recycling programs and their growing popularity, however, recycling has not solved the garbage problem. It is undisputed, for example, that recycling has not reduced the total amount of municipal wastes being generated by Americans. As conservationist Helen Spiegelman acknowledges, "Even after the enormous exertions of America's cities and towns to recycle bottles, cans, newspapers and other consumer products, seventy percent of the products we buy are still going to landfills and incinerators."[18] And recycling has no effect on how products are produced or packaged by manufacturers. As journalist and filmmaker Heather Rogers explains:

> Recycling treats wastes only after they've already been made. It does nothing to stem rubbish production in the first place. Recycling has contributed to a scaling back in the demands of the public and environmentalists by convincing us that it will remedy the situation. What gets left out of the discussion are more radical calls for things like increased product durability and serviceability, which together with less packaging would drastically cut garbage output. Recycling should be part of a larger plan, but it's not a viable solution on its own.[19]

Plastic containers are shown in a recycle basket. Plastic is the hardest material to recycle.

In fact, one of the most widely used industrial materials—plastics—is also the hardest to recycle. The use of plastics in manufacturing, to make everything from beverage containers, household items, carpets, and furniture to plastic bags and packaging materials, has caused plastics to become an increasingly large part of the municipal solid waste (MSW) stream in recent decades. According to the EPA, "In 2007, the United States generated almost 14 million tons of plastics in the MSW stream as containers and packaging, almost 7 million tons as nondurable goods, and about 10 million tons as durable goods."[20] This amounted to 12.1 percent of total MSW generation in 2007.

RECYCLING NOT A UNIVERSAL GOOD

"Recycling is a manufacturing process, and therefore it too has an environmental impact. . . . Recycling changes the nature of pollution, sometimes increasing it and sometimes decreasing it."—Daniel K. Benjamin, economics professor and former adviser to President Ronald Reagan.

Daniel K. Benjamin, "Eight Great Myths of Recycling," Property and Environment Research Center, September 2003, p. 17. www.perc.org/pdf/ps28 pdf.

The largest categories of plastic wastes include containers (for foods, drinks, and cosmetic and household items), product packaging, durable goods such as appliances and furniture, and nondurable goods such as baby diapers, trash bags, cups and utensils, and medical devices. Although 37 percent of PET bottles and 28 percent of HDPE bottles were recycled in 2007, this represents only a tiny fraction of all plastics in the waste stream. In fact, according to the EPA, only 6.8 percent of all plastic wastes generated in 2007 were recycled; the rest was buried in landfills.

Moreover, those plastics that are recycled are often made into products that cannot themselves be recycled, so recycling of plastics really only delays the time when the material ends up in a landfill. Recycled PET and HDPE plastics, for example, are typically used to make items that generally cannot be recycled at the end of their product life. As reporter Emily Gurnon explains:

All in all, plastic recycling appears to fall far short of its promise. Even if recycled under the best of conditions, a plastic bottle or margarine tub will probably have only one additional life. Since it can't be made into another food container, your Snapple bottle will become a "durable good," such as carpet or fiberfill for a jacket. Your milk bottle will become a plastic toy or the outer casing on a cell phone. Those things, in turn, will eventually be thrown away.[21]

Critics of recycling have also claimed government recycling programs are not cost-effective. In fact, the mega-landfills have actually created an abundance of space for burying trash, making landfill disposal less expensive than running recycling programs for some cities. New York mayor Michael Bloomberg, for example, canceled his city's glass and plastic recycling program in 2002 to save money, until the complaints of angry citizens caused him to partially reinstate it in 2003.

No Profit from Recycling

"Analyses typically show that recycling does not pay from a private economic point of view."—Bjorn Lomborg, a Danish author, academic, and environmental writer.

Bjorn Lomborg, *The Skeptical Environmentalist: Measuring the Real State of the World.* New York: Cambridge University Press, 2001, p. 209.

A few critics also challenge the idea that recycling is beneficial to the environment. Professor Daniel Benjamin, for example, claims that recycling itself is a manufacturing process that uses trucks and facilities and that produces greenhouse gases and other pollution just like other industries. He argues: "Curbside recycling . . . uses huge amounts of capital and labor per pound of material recycled. . . . The bulk of all curbside recycling programs simply waste resources."[22] And according to Benjamin's view, modern municipal landfills are a safe alternative to recycling. He notes that the "EPA has concluded that landfills constructed according to agency regulations can be expected to cause a total of

[only] 5.7 cancer-related deaths over the next 300 years."[23] It is the improper or illegal dumping of industrial wastes that is the real problem, he says, and recycling has no effect on these wastes.

Nor is there always a market for recycled goods. As Heather Rogers explains: "Recycled substances have to compete with 'virgin' raw materials for industrial buyers. Thanks to the billions of dollars in subsidies that extractive industries in the U.S. receive, virgin resources can often be cheaper than recycled. And when there's no market for recyclables, they become garbage."[24] Indeed, Rogers argues that the recycling solution is inherently flawed because trash is an essential part of our economic system:

> Garbage . . . is the lifeblood of capitalism. Ever more consumption is what keeps our economic system moving forward. Capitalist growth and profitability depend as much on the destruction of wealth as on the production of it. While salvaging the value contained in a discarded but perfectly usable desk is rational from an environmental and social point of view, it is irrational and not useful for the furniture industry, which must produce and sell more and more desks in order to thrive. Ultimately, the environmental crisis, of which garbage is just a subset, is inseparable from the logic of our whole economic system.[25]

The Future for Recycling

Many supporters, however, think that recycling will continue to expand, just as it has over recent decades. They believe the United States clearly has not reached its recycling limit when 70 percent of our trash is still discarded. As the NRDC says, "Since Japan, Germany, France, Sweden, Switzerland, the Netherlands, and Italy all recycle higher percentages of their wastes than does the United States, it is clear we could be doing better."[26] To boost recycling rates, the NRDC believes it is critical to improve the management of our electronic waste such as old computers, cell phones, and TVs—the fastest-growing element of the waste stream. In addition, environmentalists propose banning the use of plastic shopping bags, which now are either dumped into landfills by the billions or littered as plastic pollution in cities, rural areas, and the oceans. The city of San Francisco banned the distribution of plastic bags by grocery stores in 2007, and many other communities are considering doing the same. Also, stores around the country are encouraging shoppers to reduce plastic bag use by offering reusable bags for sale.

SORTING TRASH AS A MORAL ACT

"Sorting trash for recycling—which people used to do for money —has become a moral act, a symbol of care about the environment." —Susan Strasser, a historian of American consumer culture.

Susan Strasser, *Waste and Want: A Social History of Trash.* New York: Metropolitan, 1999, p. 293.

Yet environmental groups believe that recycling actions by consumers alone will not be enough. Many advocates, for example, propose expanding state container deposit laws, which require companies to take back the bottles used for their drink products, in order to increase the recycling of bottles and cans. Some experts also support expanding this idea to require producers of other types of products to take back, or recycle, their products at the end of their useful lives. In certain countries in Europe and in the Canadian province of British Columbia, for example, governments have begun adopting a waste policy known as Extended Producer Responsibility, or EPR, to require any company that sells a consumer product to provide cradle-to-grave take-back service to its customers. Helen Spiegelman describes the policy as it has been implemented in British Columbia:

> In British Columbia these laws are being introduced one product category at a time. First the producers of paint were called to the table and required to set up a program to take back and recycle their products from consumers. Then the producers of pesticides, pharmaceuticals, fuels, and paint thinners. Then beverage producers. Most recently the producers of packaged motor oil and oil filters.

The Recycling Content Symbol

The internationally recognized U.S. symbol for recycling—three arrows traveling in a triangle—was developed in the 1970s. During this period, many Americans were becoming concerned about the environment, and a producer of paper products—the Container Corporation of America—decided to publicize the fact that its products were manufactured using content that was recycled or recyclable. As part of this promotion, the company sponsored a nationwide art contest for a design that would signify recycling. The winner of the contest and an award of a $2,500 tuition scholarship was a twenty-three-year-old student from the University of Southern California at Los Angeles, Gary Dean Anderson. Anderson's design was influenced by the Möbius strip—a geometric shape that forms a continuous loop having only one side and one edge. Over the years, several variations of Anderson's design have been developed, and today the most common version is the one used by the U.S. plastics industry to surround the resin identification codes for plastic products. Other countries have developed different recycling symbols; Germany, for example uses a green dot symbol on plastics, and Japan employs a variety of arrow symbols to classify different recyclable materials.

The U.S. recycling symbol was developed in the 1970s by a twenty-three-year-old student named Gary Dean Anderson.

Soon it will be tires and batteries. Then British Columbia will likely follow Europe's example and require EPR for electronic products.[27]

Recycling advocates believe that making producers more responsible for recycling will not only dramatically cut down on the amount of trash going into landfills, but also encourage manufacturers to use more organic and easily recyclable materials to make their products in the first place. The response from manufacturers has been mixed: Although some industry critics have complained about this government interference with private business, other industries see economic benefits to conserving resources and reducing disposal costs.

An employee at PCC Natural Market in Seattle bags groceries into a customer's cloth bag. Many environmentalists are in favor of banning plastic bags, and many stores around the country offer reusable bags for sale to discourage the use of plastic bags.

Ideally, supporters of recycling would like to see a global recycling system, to allow products to be recycled according to a unified system around the world. The beginnings of such a system are already taking root in Europe. Germany has developed a recycling program known as the Green Dot system, in which manufacturers and retailers have to pay for a green "dot" on products. The fees charged for Green Dot increase with the amount of packaging, and monies from this program are used to help recycle the packaging. Consumers are encouraged to buy products that have the Green Dots. According to most reports, this system has led to led to a dramatic decrease in the amount of packaging used, thus creating less garbage to be recycled. Germany claims the result has been a decline of about 1 million tons (907,185 metric tons) less garbage than normal every year.

Since the Green Dot program was first implemented in Germany in 1991, it has been adopted by 22 European Union countries, as well as Norway, Latvia, the Czech Republic, and Hungary. Now used by more than 130,000 companies on 460 billion packages, the Green Dot is the most widely used trademark in the world. For many, it provides hope that the world can begin to control and reduce the seemingly endless stream of waste that humans produce in the form of product packaging. However, packaging is only one of the many challenges involved in modern waste management; perhaps even more significant is the issue of hazardous waste.

DEALING WITH
HAZARDOUS WASTE

One of the biggest problems with modern trash is that it includes not only organic biodegradable trash and nonbiodegradable materials such as plastics, but also truly hazardous substances. Hazardous waste encompasses poisonous household items and toxic industrial chemicals, as well as special types of particularly hazardous substances such as nuclear wastes and e-waste—products such as old computers, cell phones, and other electronics. U.S. laws impose special requirements for the proper disposal and cleanup of much of this hazardous waste, but certain types of hazardous substances still escape the reach of federal and state regulations.

Household Hazardous Wastes

Consumers often fail to realize that many household items contain highly dangerous ingredients that are considered hazardous wastes. According to the EPA, hazardous waste is "waste that is dangerous or potentially harmful to our health or the environment,"[28] and substances are considered hazardous if they are toxic, flammable, corrosive, or reactive. Many household products, including pesticides and commonly used cleaners, are toxic enough to cause cancer or other serious illnesses. Warnings such as "poison," "caution," "harmful or fatal if swallowed," or "use only in a well-ventilated area" on product labels are a sure sign of toxicity. In addition, many products used in the home are flammable, including paint, paint thinners, other solvents, and auto products such as motor oil, antifreeze, gasoline, brake fluid, degreasers, and cleaners. Flammable products are usually labeled with warnings such as "do not use near heat or flame," "combustible," or "do not smoke while using this product."

Other common household products are highly corrosive, meaning they contain acids or similar substances that can eat through other materials. Among these are oven cleaners, drain cleaners, toilet bowl cleaners, auto batteries, or other products with labels such as "causes severe burns on contact" or "can burn eyes, skin, throat." Reactive products refer to those that can spontaneously ignite or create poisonous vapors when mixed with other products or can explode when exposed to heat, air, water, or shock. Only a few consumer products fit this definition, such as fireworks, but mixing common household products can cause dangerous reactions. For example, mixing ordinary ammonia with chlorine bleach creates a highly toxic gas.

Experts recommend using safer alternatives for most household jobs. Simple white vinegar diluted with water is very effective for cleaning windows and other surfaces; baking soda does

Various toxic cleaning supplies are pictured underneath a kitchen sink. Many household items contain highly dangerous ingredients that are toxic enough to cause illness.

a good job of scouring sinks, toilets, and bathtubs; and ordinary soap and water can clean most clothes and carpets. Of course, shoppers today can also find many safe, so-called green household products on grocery shelves.

If consumers must use a hazardous household product, they can reduce their risks by reading the labels, carefully following label directions, and storing these products away from children and pets. State and local laws vary, but it is still legal in most areas for homeowners to throw household hazardous substances into the trash. Environmental advocates, however, urge that these items instead should be brought to a local hazardous waste collection site, where they can be handled properly and kept out of the environment.

100 POUNDS OF WASTE PER HOUSEHOLD

"The average home can accumulate as much as 100 pounds of HHW [household hazardous waste] in the basement and garage and in storage closets."—U.S. Environmental Protection Agency.

U.S. Environmental Protection Agency, "Household Hazardous Waste." www.epa.gov/osw/conserve/materials/hhw.htm.

In addition, many consumer appliances and electronics contain hazardous substances. Old refrigerators and air conditioners, for example, contain chlorofluorocarbons (CFCs)—chemical pollutants that under the federal Clean Air Act cannot be released into the atmosphere. It is important to recycle these appliances to ensure that the CFCs are safely removed. Other hazardous items commonly found in the home include batteries, car tires, and electronic products such as printers, computers, cell phones, and TVs. Like refrigerators, these items should never be dumped into the trash or regular recycling, but should be taken to hazardous waste sites or to specially designated drop-off sites.

Industrial Hazardous Wastes

Hazardous industrial wastes pose even more risk than hazardous household products. Some hazardous wastes produced by manufacturing are solid and easily contained; other hazardous industrial wastes are gases that can escape into the air or liquids that can contaminate groundwater supplies. Industrial operations in developed nations such as the United States have produced large quantities of hazardous waste for multiple decades, and most of that time, the disposal of these wastes was either totally unregulated or enforcement of government regulations was lax. For many years, companies simply vented gaseous wastes into the atmosphere and loaded solid and liquid toxic chemical, plastic, or pesticide wastes into large metal drums and dumped them either above or under the ground.

The danger of hazardous industrial wastes to human health and the environment was first brought home to Americans in the 1970s when an environmental disaster unfolded at Love Canal, an industrial dump site in the city of Niagara Falls, New York. The canal was owned by Hooker Chemical Company, a subsidiary of Occidental Petroleum. For thirty-three years, from

This is an aerial view of the community where toxic waste was dumped by the Hooker Chemical Company into the Love Canal in Niagara Falls, New York.

1920 until 1953, Hooker used the dump site, filling it with more than 21,000 tons (19,051 metric tons) of chemicals—many of them now known to be potent carcinogens. Among these were pesticides such as lindane and DDT, multiple solvents, polychlorinated biphenyls (PCBs), dioxin, and heavy metals.

A HEAVY METAL STEW

"The [sewage] sludge being spread on our crop fields is a dangerous stew of heavy metals, industrial compounds, viruses, bacteria, drug residues, and radioactive material."—Center for Food Safety.

Center for Food Safety, "Sewage Sludge." www.centerforfoodsafety.org/sewage_slu.cfm.

In 1953, after filling the canal and covering it over with soil, Hooker sold the land for one dollar to the Niagara Falls Board of Education, which constructed an elementary school and a playground nearby. Homes were also built along the canal, and by 1978 the area had 800 single-family homes and 240 low-income apartments, and about 400 children attended the local elementary school.

Residents of Love Canal became alarmed as trees and gardens started dying, drums of chemicals began surfacing and leaching into backyards and basements, and children experienced recurring infections and leukemia. Residents also exhibited lesions and burns and had high rates of miscarriages and birth defects; later, blood tests showed precancerous conditions in many adults. The community eventually discovered that their neighborhood was sitting on a massive industrial dump, and local activists began an uphill battle to show that the chemicals buried in the canal were responsible for their health problems.

Both Hooker and the local government at first denied any responsibility, but finally in 1978, President Jimmy Carter declared a federal emergency at Love Canal. After more investigation, a second emergency was declared in 1980. Ultimately, the federal government relocated more than 900 families and reimbursed them for their homes. In 1995, after the EPA sued Occidental Petroleum, the company agreed to pay $129 million in restitution. The events at Love Canal marked an awakening of the American public to the health consequences of environmental contamination with industrial chemicals and led to federal legislation regulating industrial hazardous wastes.

Today, according to the EPA, "American industrial facilities generate and dispose of approximately 7.6 billion tons of industrial solid waste each year . . . from 17 different industry groups."[29] Of this total, the EPA reports that approximately 46.7 million tons (42.4 million metric tons) consists of hazardous wastes as defined by the U.S. government. However, the actual amount of industrial hazardous waste produced in the United States is probably much larger, because the EPA's data consist only of information obtained from companies that generated large quantities of industrial hazardous wastes; smaller producers of hazardous wastes are not counted by the government. In addition, environmental advocates assert that an unknown number of companies engage in illegal dumping of hazardous wastes in order to avoid the costs of proper disposal.

Agricultural Hazardous Wastes

Industrial manufacturing is not the only industry that generates hazardous wastes, however. Enormous amounts of hazardous chemical pesticides and herbicides are used on crops by U.S. agriculture producers each year. Many of these chemicals run off into the soil and groundwater, and any materials left over are considered hazardous wastes. In some cases, too, the application of phosphate fertilizer produces fluoride wastes. Even animal manure produces concentrated nitrates that can leach into groundwater, contaminate drinking-water wells, and cause health problems.

Moreover, many farms recycle and use industrial hazardous wastes as fertilizers because, in addition to toxins, they contain nutrients such as nitrogen, phosphorus, and potassium that are beneficial to plants. As reporter Patty Martin explains:

> Each year, approximately 110 billion pounds of fertilizer are applied to farm fields throughout the U.S. Unfortunately, almost one-half of that total is non-nutrient material of unknown composition. The fertilizer industry has

acknowledged that about 150 million pounds of hazardous waste end up in the agricultural system each year—wastes from steel mills, tanneries, film processors, and coal-fired power plants that are "recycled," supposedly to provide some benefits to crops without regard for the contaminants "along for the ride." Some of these wastes carry toxins such as mercury, lead, cadmium, arsenic, uranium, nickel, chromium, and dioxins.[30]

This use of hazardous waste in fertilizer, critics say, is permissible because of loopholes in current EPA regulations and many state regulatory systems.

Another fertilizer source is sewage sludge, which may contain dangerous levels of pathogens, as well as PCBs, chlorinated pesticides, asbestos, industrial solvents, petroleum products, radioactive

A farmer inspects a dead patch of a field caused by sewage sludge used as a fertilizer. Many farms like this one use industrial hazardous wastes as fertilizers because, in addition to toxins, they contain nutrients that are beneficial to plants. One fertilizer source in particular is sewage sludge, which may contain dangerous levels of pathogens.

material, and heavy metals. And these toxins can also be found in some fertilizers sold for use in home gardens because these products do not have to be labeled to reveal their hazardous content.

The agriculture industry claims that toxic materials are not being absorbed into food products, but critics believe otherwise. They point to dramatic increases in the amount of arsenic in toddlers' diets, as well as increases in asthma, cancers, birth defects, and developmental disabilities—all of which are increasingly thought to be linked to environmental toxins found in the human food chain.

Regulation of Hazardous Wastes

Hazardous waste was first addressed in federal law in 1965 with the passage of the Solid Waste Disposal Act, which sought to segregate hazardous materials from other solid wastes to prevent soil and groundwater contamination. In 1976, after PCBs—chemicals used in the insulation of electrical equipment—were found to cause cancer, Congress passed the Toxic Substances Control Act to regulate the use, management, and disposal of PCBs and certain other toxic substances.

In 1976, however, the United States began more comprehensively regulating the treatment, storage, and disposal of hazardous wastes with the passage of the Resource Conservation and Recovery Act (RCRA). In the 1984 reauthorization of RCRA, Congress added the Hazardous and Solid Waste Amendments. The RCRA basically sets up a cradle-to-grave system of record keeping for hazardous wastes and regulates the manner in which they should be disposed. Under the law, hazardous wastes—whether solid, liquid, or gas—must be tracked from the time they are generated until their final disposal.

The RCRA divides hazardous wastes into three categories. The first category covers materials subject to full hazardous waste regulations. These include materials that contain one of thirty-nine carcinogenic substances, catch fire easily (such as gasoline, solvents, and paints), could explode or release toxic fumes (such as acids, ammonia, chlorine bleach), or are capable of corroding metal containers such as tanks, drums, and barrels (such as industrial cleaning agents and oven and drain cleaners). A second

Deep well injection is one way of disposing of hazardous industrial waste. A wastewater plant in Florida has thirteen underground injection wells that pump wastewater into limestone caverns below the earth.

category applies to materials that are subject to less stringent requirements, such as oil, batteries, fluorescent lightbulbs, pesticides, and thermostats (materials containing mercury).

Category three under the RCRA refers to materials that are exempted from its solid waste definition. Exempted materials, or materials not included in the law's definition of hazardous wastes, include household wastes, domestic sewage, wastes that pass through a publicly owned treatment plant, irrigation water, industrial wastes recycled as fertilizers, mining wastes that are left in the ground, recycled sulfuric acid, wastes from the burning of coal or other fossil fuels, and chromium wastes. In addition, some industrial discharges are otherwise regulated by the Clean Water Act or Clean Air Act, radioactive wastes are specifically controlled by the Atomic Energy Act of 1954, and medical wastes are governed by the Medical Waste Tracking Act of 1988.

The RCRA requires companies that generate hazardous wastes to dispose of them in special ways to decrease their health and environmental risks. Today about 60 percent of all hazardous industrial waste in the United States is disposed of using a method called deep well injection. This method injects liquid wastes into a well located in a type of nonporous rock formation that keeps the waste isolated from groundwater and surface water. Other hazardous wastes are disposed of using specially designed landfills and high-temperature incinerators.

Superfund Sites

Following the Love Canal disaster, Congress also passed the Comprehensive Environmental Response, Compensation, and Liability Act of 1980 (CERCLA) to clean up past hazardous waste disposal sites. The act was funded by corporate taxes in order to create a government fund, which came to be known as "Superfund," to pay for cleaning hazardous sites. Under the law, abandoned and particularly dangerous waste sites may qualify as Superfund sites, eligible for government cleanup. CERCLA was reauthorized in 1986 with the Superfund Amendments and Reauthorization Act.

Superfund Megasites

Almost three decades after Congress passed the Comprehensive Environmental Response, Compensation, and Liability Act of 1980 (CERCLA) to clean up the nation's most dangerous hazardous waste dumps, the nation still has a long list of "Superfund megasites"—places that are so polluted with chemicals and toxins that experts expect they will cost more than $50 million each to clean up. As of 2007, 154 locations had been named megasites, and the list continues to grow as more mines, landfills, and factories qualify. One of these sites is in southern California, off the Palos Verdes Peninsula, where a large deposit of the pesticide DDT on the ocean floor has been poisoning fish and other marine life for decades. Another megasite in Butte, Montana, is a 900-foot-deep (274m), open-air pit of toxic waste left over from an old copper mine; the pit is so huge that it has become a tourist attraction. Polluters pay for most Superfund cleanups, but cleanups of megasites have become increasingly more expensive, often as much as $140 million or more for each site. Yet Superfund's annual budget has remained at about $1.2 billion since the program began, making big cleanups ever harder to finance.

Since the passage of the Superfund law, hundreds of hazardous waste sites have been cleaned up, but many others are still awaiting decontamination. During the initial period following CERCLA's passage, the EPA first conducted thirty-three hundred emergency removals—urgent cleanups of hazardous wastes because of the immediate hazard they presented to public health or the environment. In 1993 the EPA inventoried about 38,000 remaining sites, selecting from these a list of the most dangerous sites, officially placing them on the Superfund National Priorities List. As of 2008 this list consisted of 1,317 sites.

Hazardous waste sites are cleaned using a variety of physical, chemical, or biological methods. A few types of wastes can be treated simply by diluting them with water. Others react positively to chemicals; for example, the chemical sodium hydroxide has been used to treat acid wastes. Infectious medical wastes are typically incinerated. Liquid hazardous wastes are sometimes solidified by mixing them with other materials, so that they harden and no longer pose a risk for underground water systems. Yet another method is building a physical barrier around waste matter; this barrier might be made of plastic, steel, concrete, clay, or glass. The most difficult type of hazardous waste to remedy is gaseous

An EPA Quanta Resources Superfund Site sign is posted in a hazardous vacant lot. Government funds, known as "Superfund," pay for the cleanup of hazardous sites that are eligible.

plumes that are emitted from some hazardous waste dumps. Sometimes, these plumes can be confined by drilling wells around the area and injecting them with water to block the escape of hazardous gases. In the case of chlorinated solvent gases, the area can be surrounded with a trench that contains powdered iron, which can react with the hazardous gases and turn them into less hazardous hydrocarbons.

Nuclear Wastes

Special issues arise with certain categories of hazardous wastes. For example, nuclear waste presents serious political and technical problems for which there are few satisfactory answers. Some low-level radioactive wastes are produced by the use of relatively small amounts of radioactive materials for electricity generation, medical diagnosis and treatment, biomedical and pharmaceutical research, and some forms of manufacturing. Also, the end of the Cold War—the period of ideological tension between the United States and the Soviet Union from 1945 to 1991—left both countries with high-level radioactive waste from decommissioned nuclear weapons. However, most high-level radioactive wastes are created when uranium is mined for use as nuclear fuel, or later when nuclear power plants produce spent fuel that is highly radioactive.

Mining, for example, separates relatively small amounts of uranium ore from vast layers of impervious rock, creating tailings —a liquid, radioactive mud that can decay into radium-226, which in turn decays into radon gas, a potent carcinogen. Once released by the mining process, these tailings can pollute waterways or drift into the air and can persist in the environment for up to one hundred thousand years. Many uranium mining sites have become environmental wastelands, unfit for human habitation. Some abandoned uranium mines are located in Australia, while others can be found in the southwestern United States. Most of the uranium wastelands, however, are located in the poor African countries of Namibia and Niger, where they continue to cause devastating health problems for local peoples.

Nuclear reactors, used to produce electricity, also create tons of radioactive nuclear wastes. Reactors must be closed down every year or so to replace about one-third of their uranium fuel rods. Each time, this creates about 30 tons (27 metric tons) of spent fuel made up of plutonium, fission products, and uranium —all of which emit lethal radiation. In fact, as University of Rochester engineer Ezra Gold notes, "The toxicity of plutonium is among the highest of any element known."[31] This material is stored in water-cooled ponds at the reactor site for at least fifteen days, allowing the radioactivity to drop significantly. Afterward, however, the spent fuel remains a dangerous, slowly decaying radioactive material for thousands of years.

Low-level radioactive wastes are fairly easily disposed of, usually by encapsulating them in heavy concrete containers or vaults, which are then buried deep underground. These wastes lose most of their radioactive risks after a few decades. So far, however, no one has found a viable, permanent disposal solution for high-level radioactive wastes that stay radioactive virtually forever.

The Yucca Mountain Controversy

The disposal of nuclear hazardous wastes is one of the most controversial issues in U.S. waste management policy. In 1982 Congress enacted the Nuclear Waste Policy Act, which directed the U.S. Department of Energy to build a deep geologic repository for high-level radioactive waste no later than 1998. In 1987 Congress amended the act to propose Yucca Mountain, Nevada—a remote desert location— as the site for this national nuclear repository. However, years of delays have extended the 1998 deadline more than 20 years; the facility is not expected to open until at least 2020, if it ever opens at all.

The delays were caused by strong opposition from Nevada citizens and political leaders, who did not want their state to become the dumping ground for highly dangerous wastes. The repository site is also situated on land claimed by a Native American tribe, the Western Shoshone Nation. After numerous lawsuits, Congress and President George W. Bush finally approved the Yucca Mountain site in 2002. If it is built, the facility will house over 77,160 tons (70,000 metric tons) of highly radioactive waste, most of it from U.S. nuclear reactors, where it has been piling up in temporary storage containers.

Many uranium mining sites, like the abandoned open pit uranium mine shown here, have become environmental wastelands.

Most countries that operate nuclear reactors have opted for one of three methods: storing it in containers on the earth's surface, burying it deep in the ground in containers, or reprocessing it into solid glass or ceramic blocks for deep burial.

The storage of nuclear wastes at nuclear plants, critics say, raises concerns about potential terrorist strikes or accidental release of radioactive materials. The nuclear industry, for its part, favors deep burial of wastes into geological formations of granite or basalt—materials believed to be hard enough to prevent movement of the wastes —sealed with concrete. Yet this option also has its weaknesses, because natural events such as earthquakes or volcanic activity can disrupt rock formations and potentially disturb and release radioactive wastes into the environment. Another issue involved in burying nuclear waste is that people, understandably, do not want burial sites located anywhere close to where they live. A huge and prolonged political controversy has arisen in the United States, for example, over Yucca Mountain —a remote desert site in Nevada selected by the government to be a repository for all of the nation's nuclear wastes.

E-Wastes

The rapid advances in technology in the past few decades have created a new hazardous waste problem—the discarding of consumer electronics, called e-waste, which contain numerous toxic materials.

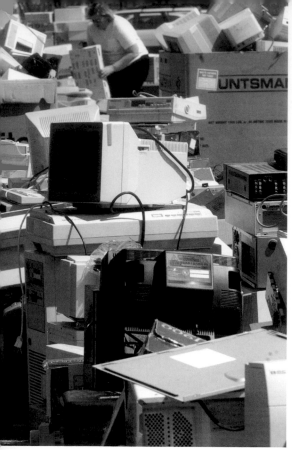

Used computer gear fills a waste collection lot. A new hazardous problem has emerged that is referred to as e-waste. E-waste is highly hazardous, so there are many concerns over how to discard it.

As the Electronics TakeBack Coalition notes, "Discarded computers, monitors, televisions, and other consumer electronics (so called e-waste) are the fastest growing portion of our waste stream."[32] According to the EPA, "In 2007, discarded TVs, computers, peripherals (including printers, scanners, faxes), mice, keyboards and cell phones totaled about 2.5 million tons [in the United States]."[33] Yet only about 18 percent of U.S. computers and TVs and only about 10 percent of cell phones were recycled in 2007. Worldwide, the United Nations Environment Programme estimates that 22 to 55 million tons (20 to 50 million metric tons) of e-waste are generated each year, and other estimates have ranged as high as 441 million tons (400 million metric tons).

FASTEST GROWING WASTE PROBLEM

"[E-waste is] the world's fastest growing and potentially most dangerous waste problem."—Chris Prystay.

Chris Prystay, "Recycling E-waste," *Wall Street Journal*, September 23, 2004, p. B1.

The main concern with e-waste is its highly hazardous content. As the Electronics TakeBack Coalition explains: "Over 1,000 materials, including chlorinated solvents, brominated flame retardants, PVC [a type of plastic], heavy metals, plastics and gases, are used to make electronic products and their components—semiconductor chips, circuit boards, and disk drives."[34] Computer monitors, for example, often contain 4 to 8 pounds (1.8 to 3.6 kg) of lead—a heavy metal known to cause brain damage in children—and big-screen TVs have even more lead content. Flat-panel TVs also use large amounts of mercury, a toxin that is carcinogenic even in very tiny doses; as little as 0.014 teaspoons (0.07mL) can pollute an entire lake. In addition, brominated flame retardants are widely used in plastic cases and cables for fire retardancy, and the heavy metal cadmium was widely used for years in rechargeable batteries for laptops and other portable electronics. Most newer rechargeable batteries do not contain cadmium. Much of this e-waste is produced by rich nations but exported to developing countries for disposal, where the absence of government regulations often exposes poor workers to health hazards and pollutes the local environment.

E-WASTE STILL A SMALL PROBLEM

"While the amount of e-waste has been increasing, it remains a tiny percent of the total municipal solid waste stream."—Dana Joel Gattuso.

Dana Joel Gattuso, "Mandated Recycling of Electronics: A Lose-Lose Proposition," *Issue Analysis*, February 1, 2005. http://cei.org/gencon/025,04386.cfm.

The hazardous e-waste stream is expected to explode to even greater proportions in the future, as technology continues its relentless advance. In the United States, because of a federal requirement that all TV signals switch to digital in June 2009, many older TVs will become obsolete and will likely be trashed, adding significantly to the volume of e-wastes. And in future decades, developing nations are expected to add billions of new electronics consumers to the world market, creating unknown amounts of additional e-waste and adding to what is becoming a global garbage challenge.

WASTE MANAGEMENT— A GLOBAL CHALLENGE

Because wastes are generated everywhere, garbage presents a challenge around the globe, in both developed and poor countries, as well as in common areas such as the world's oceans. Waste management strategies vary from country to country, but most countries that can afford it employ some combination of the same methods used in the United States—source reduction, incineration, recycling, and landfills. Rapid development in certain countries such as India and China, along with ever-increasing global population growth, is expected to produce continuing waste management issues into the future.

Waste Management in Europe

Most developed countries face the same problems with trash as the United States. In fact, some areas of the globe are way ahead of the United States in trash technology and policies. Europe, for example, due to its dense population, began running out of landfill space long ago. Many European countries turned to incinerators, but this method has become increasingly disfavored because it produces too much air pollution and hazardous waste. As a result, some countries in Europe have begun implementing strategies to eliminate large amounts of garbage that would otherwise have to be burned or dumped. Thanks to the adoption of packaging and bottle-return laws, the use of new trash technologies, and the resort to aggressive recycling programs, Europeans now generate only half as much trash per person as Americans.

The European Union (EU), a group of twenty-seven mostly European nations, has been instrumental in encouraging more effective waste management policies. In 1994, for example, the

European Union issued a Packaging and Packaging Waste Directive aimed at reducing the amount of trash going to landfills and incinerators. The directive encourages minimization of the amount of material used in packaging, the reuse of packaging components, and recycling of packaging materials. Another EU directive, called Waste Electrical and Electronic Equipment, seeks to create systems for the collection, treatment, and recycling of electronic wastes. The EU also has directed member nations to reduce the amount of trash sent to landfills to 35 percent of what it was in 1995 by the year 2020.

However, some European countries have developed much more advanced waste management policies than others. Greece, for example, is far behind most other European countries in terms of reducing wastes and implementing recycling. Each year, the country sends about 90 percent of its trash to landfills, including about a billion plastic drinking water bottles, another billion soft drink bottles, and yet another billion plastic containers for cleaning fluids. Only

Germany is a recycling leader in Europe. The country encourages recycling through the use of seven recycling bins, four of which are pictured here.

Restmüll   Verpackung   Glas   Papier

about 1 percent of Greek plastic waste is recycled. Italy is another European country that struggles with waste issues. In 2008 Naples, a city in southern Italy, became the poster child for the nation's garbage problems when mountains of rotting trash were allowed to pile up on city streets because the country had run out of landfill space. Eventually, in the summer of 2008, the crisis was temporarily solved when Naples's trash was sent by train to incinerators in Hamburg, Germany. The European Commission, the executive body of the EU, filed suit against Italy in May 2008 for failing to meet its obligation to collect and dispose of garbage. Garbage problems also afflict Spain, France, and Ireland, which a recent study found are unlikely to meet the long-term EU targets for trash reduction.

The United Kingdom, too, has long had a bad reputation for ineffective waste management and recycling, although it has made some progress in recent years. In 1997 the nation recycled just 7 percent of its waste, but today it recycles close to 30 percent —a figure close to the U.S. recycling rate. Yet the United Kingdom still faces huge waste management challenges. As Nick Mann of the British Local Government Association explains, "We have described the U.K. as the dustbin of Europe because we put more to landfill than any other country in the EU, and our landfill space is running out very quickly."[35] In fact, British wastes are increasing 3 percent a year, and its dumps are expected to be filled to capacity in only nine more years.

At the other end of the spectrum, Germany, Belgium, Sweden, and Luxembourg all send less than a quarter of their trash to landfills. These countries over the last decade have developed various strategies to reduce and properly dispose of their waste, such as closing polluting landfills and investing in high-volume recycling and trash reduction programs. They also have built state-of-the-art incinerators that minimize air pollution with filters and that capture energy for use in heating homes and water.

Germany, for example, is one of the leaders in Europe on recycling and the environment. The entire country is encouraged to recycle waste into seven bins—yellow for packaging materials; blue for paper and cardboard; three bins for clear, brown, and green glass; a "Bio" bin for leftover food and other organic wastes;

and a black bin for everything else. Germans are required to take special items such as batteries or chemicals to a recycling center. Failure to recycle properly can result in a nasty note, or even a fine, from the local waste management company. The country's modern recycling centers then employ technological advances such as precision, computer-guided infrared scanners to separate and compact recycled materials into different types of neat bales, which are sold for profit. Germans also pay a plastic bottle deposit, which is refunded when the bottles are returned to the stores where the products were purchased.

Recycling Plastics Is a Dirty Job

"The majority of the plastics we recycle . . . end up in China, where worker safety standards are virtually nonexistent and materials are processed under dirty, primitive conditions."—Emily Gurnon, a writer and reporter who has written for the *San Francisco Examiner*, the *Los Angeles Times*, and other newspapers.

Emily Gurnon, "The Problem with Plastics: Recycling It Overseas Poses Risks to Workers. Doing It Here Doesn't Pay," Mindfully.org, June 5, 2003. www.mindfully.org/Plastic/Recycling/Problem-With-Plastics5jun03.htm.

These waste reduction strategies have paid off. As reporter Andreas Tzortzis explains, "One of Europe's recycling pioneers, Germany has steadily increased the amount of glass, paper, plastic and packaging products it recycles from around 11 million tons in 1995 to more than 15 million in 2005."[36] Germany now recycles more than 75 percent of its garbage, and what it cannot recycle is incinerated in high-tech facilities and used to generate energy.

Garbage Challenges in Developing Countries

The problems of waste management are different for the developing world. Because the economies of developing countries are usually not as robust as the economies of countries such as the United States, people in these poorer countries tend to buy fewer products with less packaging, and they produce less waste than Americans or residents of other industrialized nations. On the

A child scavenges on a dump in Manila, in the Philippines. Many developing countries have problems disposing of wastes. As a result, garbage piles up and people scavenge through the trash to try to earn a living.

other hand, unlike developed nations, poorer countries in the developing world often have not developed adequate waste management policies or systems, trash collection services, or government institutions to properly manage their wastes. As the Web site Fabric of Nature explains:

> Most developing countries don't have any organized means of controlling solid waste. Garbage is rarely even collected on a regular basis. Regulations vary from country to country and from town to town, and often a small bribe from an apprehended illegal trash dumper will trump enforcement of official regulations, anyway. Laws are often lax—burning of garbage and open dumping allowed. Frequently, a lack of funds prevents municipalities in such countries from ever being able to even create a proper waste management system, in the first place.

Then, the lack of status and poor salaries associated with the profession discourages qualified employees, so personnel rarely has the ability or the training to manage an effective system, even when one exists.[37]

The result in many cases is that garbage in developing countries tends to pile up in waterways and on land, creating serious health and environmental hazards. This problem of waste management is especially acute in countries with rapidly growing urban areas. As World Health Organization researcher Hisashi Ogawa notes, "The management of solid waste is becoming a major public health and environmental concern in urban areas of many developing countries."[38]

A DEVELOPING COUNTRY'S TRASH

"One of the surest signs that you're in a developing country is the trash beneath your feet."—Bryan Walsh, *Time* magazine's energy and climate writer.

Bryan Walsh, "Trash Problems in Paradise," *Time*, January 2, 2008. www.time.com/time/world/article/0,8599,1701095,00.html.

One of the worst examples is the city of Manila, capital of the Philippines. There, residents generate 8,000 tons (7,982 metric tons) of garbage each day, but for years the government did not collect the garbage or educate the public about recycling or other waste reduction options. As a result, the city's garbage simply piled up at numerous dumps, which attracted flies, rats, and other vermin. The dumps also encouraged poor people to scavenge amongst the trash to earn a meager living. Some people even lived on the dumps in shanties amid fetid garbage, methane fumes, and various toxins. In 2000 one of the biggest dumps— a huge trash mountain called Payatas—collapsed after typhoon rains, destroying one of the shantytowns and killing 219 people. After the tragedy, the government cleaned up the site, but a new dump was opened next door that continues to provide the only source of income for many poor residents.

As poorer nations industrialize and become wealthier and more consumer oriented, garbage problems usually worsen. China, which has become an economic powerhouse in just the last decade, is the best example of this phenomenon. According to a 2005 World Bank report: "China recently surpassed the United States as the world's largest municipal solid waste (MSW) generator. In 2004 the urban areas of China generated about 190,000,000 tonnes of MSW and by 2030 this amount is projected to be at least 480,000,000 tonnes. No country has ever experienced as large, or as rapid, an increase in waste generation."[39]

Managing this rapid increase in garbage presents all kinds of major health, social, and environmental problems. Perhaps the worst impact in China is environmental deterioration so bad that Chinese people are regularly sickened by toxic pollutants entering the air, soil, and water. The World Bank has estimated that almost half a million Chinese people die prematurely each year from breathing in the polluted air and drinking the dirty water. Yet government efforts to address this pollution face enormous obstacles, as millions of Chinese demand their slice of the growing economic pie. As journalist David Stanway explains, "With hundreds of millions of urban residents enjoying the fruits of consumerism, the government is struggling to bring a sense of the environmental costs of breakneck economic growth. It has tried to rein in industrial polluters by cutting off credit, suspending licenses and jailing repeat offenders, but officials bemoan the failure of ordinary people to be green."[40] Some Chinese leaders have even speculated that the environmental destruction may eventually halt China's economic progress.

Trash Exports

The developing world also is the destination for much of the trash produced by rich countries. Many Western nations, including the United States, have been shipping recyclable trash overseas to foreign countries since the 1970s. Developing nations use this recyclable garbage as a source of cheap raw materials. For example, as Chinese journalist Tang Hou explains: "China is the world's second largest consumer of plastic; one ton of synthetic resin costs 11,000 yuan (around US $1,420), but a ton of imported plastic can be bought for as little as 4,000 yuan (around US $515). The work of sorting the

Garbage in Paradise

Poor, developing nations typically have a difficult time financing a system for garbage pickup and disposal. Even beautiful tropical places known as tourist destinations face this problem; outside the meticulously groomed resorts, piles of garbage often rot in the hot sun. The island of Bali, part of Indonesia, is a prime example. Bali's growing population produces more than 5,000 tons (4,536 metric tons) of garbage each day, much of it plastic bags and containers. Yet the island still has little in the way of trash services or pickup, and what is collected is dumped into a huge, unsanitary landfill. As a result, the trash piles up on riverbanks and in mangrove forests, leaching chemicals into the environment and creating a visual blight. And during the wet season, winds blow garbage from the ocean onto Bali's beaches. Resorts often hire workers to scour the tourist beaches and other areas, removing bits of trash, but outside the resorts, the only real waste management comes from scavengers who climb through garbage dumps looking for anything they can use or sell. In the future, Bali residents hope that growing public awareness and green technology will help reduce the island's garbage problem.

Even tropical locations, like the island of Bali, can have difficulties disposing of its garbage. In this photo, piles of burning garbage have been dumped next to a rice field in Bali.

waste is hard and dirty, but for many it is more lucrative than the alternative."[41] This trash trade is a growing international industry.

However, for the people living in the importing nations, there is a dark side to these trash deals. Usually, the trash is sent to countries that have few environmental or health regulations or little enforcement, allowing the foreign garbage to be handled in ways that expose local people and their lands to dangerous toxins. As China Greenpeace spokesman Jamie Choi explains: "China has become a big dumping ground for rubbish from Britain and other countries. A lot of the waste is toxic and sorted by migrant workers who are not protected from its effects."[42] British journalist Oliver Harvey describes visiting the Chinese town of Mai, known as Plastic City for its mountains of trash:

> There is a constant caustic stench amid the thick plumes of dark smoke. Dozens of factories and smaller outfits alongside ramshackle homes melt down recycled plastic. Many locals believe the pollution is ruining their health and even causing birth defects. One 25-year-old woman worker, who did not want to be named, said: "We know that it is really bad for us here. Every morning we wake up coughing to try to clear out our throats. But we have no choice—we need the work to support our families."[43]

Exporting and Importing Hazardous Wastes

Perhaps the most alarming part of the international trash trade is the growing practice of shipping hazardous wastes across national borders. In developed nations, these wastes are difficult and expensive to dispose of legally in a way that minimizes harm to the environment and to people. As a result, producers and recyclers are tempted to ship the waste to poor countries, where sometimes corrupt leaders offer much cheaper disposal fees. The problem, however, is that developing nations typically do not process the hazardous wastes properly, leading to a string of hazardous waste scandals in recent years.

In August 2006, for example, a Dutch tanker called the *Probo Koala* illegally dumped more than 500 tons (499 metric tons) of toxic sludge in the African nation of Côte d'Ivoire, sickening more

Waste is often shipped to poor countries because of lower disposal fees. However, developing nations often do not have the means to dispose of the waste properly. In 2006 the Probo Koala, *a Dutch tanker, illegally dumped toxic sludge in the African nation of Côte d'Ivoire, sickening thousands of people.*

than 40,000 people and causing 17 deaths, some of them children. The sludge contained high concentrations of mercaptan, a substance found in some crude oils that is highly toxic; it was dumped at multiple locations essential to human health—near vegetable fields, fisheries, and water reservoirs.

The wastes were dumped by Trafigura, a Dutch oil trading company with annual sales of $28 billion, which reportedly rejected a bid of $250,000 for proper disposal in the Netherlands, choosing instead to ship its wastes to Côte d'Ivoire for a relatively small fee of $18,500. As journalists Sebastian Knauer, Thilo Thielke, and Gerald Traufetter explain, "The [*Probo Koala*] disaster is instructive: This is what happens when affluent western societies run out of places to dump their waste; when increasingly stringent environmental laws at home mean skyrocketing waste disposal costs; when criminal profiteers seek low-cost solutions."[44]

The *Probo Koala* incident and other hazardous waste disasters have occurred despite the international community's attempt to control the global hazardous waste trade. In 1989 the Basel Convention on the Control of Transboundary Movements of Hazardous Wastes and Their Disposal was adopted at a meeting convened by the United Nations Environment Programme. The treaty, signed by 170 nations, sought to reduce the international transportation of hazardous wastes. However, the treaty proved to be weak, and in 1994 a coalition of countries agreed to amend the treaty to ban all forms of hazardous waste exports from the twenty-nine wealthiest, most industrialized countries of the Organization for Economic Cooperation and Development (OECD) to all non-OECD countries. Yet the battle to enforce the Basel agreement continues to the present day, in the face of strong opposition from industrial lobby groups in the United States and other developed countries. The United States has signed but not ratified the Basel agreement, and the amended treaty so far has largely failed to stop a growing illegal global trade in hazardous wastes.

Hazardous Waste Is Increasingly Dangerous

"If not addressed comprehensively, the problems of accumulating hazardous materials generated by and used in high-tech manufacturing and e-waste risk undermining the ecological sustainability of affected communities worldwide."—Elizabeth Grossman, environmental journalist and author.

Elizabeth Grossman, *High Tech Trash: Digital Devices, Hidden Toxics, and Human Health.* Washington, DC: Island, 2006, p. 263.

In fact, one of the most dangerous types of hazardous waste in the illegal stream today is e-waste, which is rapidly increasing around the world as wave after wave of technology floods the consumer markets. But developed nations have not devised adequate strategies for dealing with these electronic wastes, so much of it ends up in developing countries, where it contaminates water, soil, and air. As author Elizabeth Grossman explains:

> Over the past two decades or more, rapid technological advances have doubled the computing capacity of semiconductor chips almost every eighteen months, bringing

us faster computers, smaller cell phones, more efficient machinery and appliances, and an increasing demand for new products. Yet this rushing stream of amazing electronics leaves in its wake environmental degradation and a large volume of hazardous waste.[45]

According to some environmental advocacy groups, the United States is one of the worst offenders, exporting large amounts of hazardous e-waste to places such as China, India, and Pakistan.

Plastic Pollution in the World's Oceans

The world's trash problem has even invaded some of the most remote places on earth. The great oceans—areas once considered so vast that they could never be affected by human activities—are becoming polluted with nonbiodegradable, toxic plastics. One of the largest areas of ocean pollution is called the Great Pacific Garbage Patch—a floating mass of plastic waste located in the middle of the Pacific Ocean between California and Hawaii. According to researcher Charles Moore, who first discovered the garbage patch in 1997 during a yacht race, this pollution is growing and may already cover an area up to one and one-half times the size of the United States, to a depth of 100 feet (30m) or more. More conservative estimates say it is the size of Texas. Either way, it is a remarkable amount of garbage.

The plastic debris in the garbage patch, mostly land-based items such as plastic bags, balloons, bottles, packaging, and other materials, poses a terrible threat to birds and other marine life. As reporter Justin Berton explains: "Sea turtles mistake clear plastic bags for jellyfish. Birds swoop down and swallow indigestible shards of plastic. The petroleum-based plastics take decades to break down, and as long as they float on the ocean's surface, they can appear as feeding grounds."[46] According to Warner Chabot, vice president of the Ocean Conservancy: "Animals die because the plastic eventually fills their stomachs. . . . It doesn't pass, and they literally starve to death."[47] Plastic items such as fishnets can also ensnare sea turtles, dolphins, and other marine animals, causing injury or death. In fact, a 2006 report by the environmental group Greenpeace, "Plastic Debris in the World's Oceans,"

The world's oceans are becoming polluted with hazardous plastics. One of the largest areas of ocean pollution is called the Great Pacific Garbage Patch. The Algalita Junk raft sails from California to Hawaii to bring attention to the plastic debris situation in the Pacific.

found that at least 267 marine species had suffered from some kind of ingestion or entanglement with marine debris.

In addition, many experts fear that these plastics are making their way into the human food chain, as ocean fish eat the plastic bits, absorb chemicals and pollutants, and in turn are eaten by people. As Charles Moore's Algalita Marine Research Foundation explains: "Plastic debris releases chemical additives and plasticizers into the ocean. Plastic also absorbs hydrophobic pollutants like PCBs and pesticides like DDT. These pollutants bioaccumulate in the tissues of marine organisms, biomagnify up the food chain, and find their way into the foods we eat."[48] Studies have shown, in fact, that both people and animals around the world carry numerous industrial toxins in their bodies as a result of widespread environmental pollution.

The Future of Garbage

Whether the people of the world will be able to reduce the amount of plastics and other trash they produce or solve the problems of hazardous and toxic wastes is an open question. First, the future size of the world's waste stream will depend on a number of factors. Rising populations in some parts of the world suggest that the global trash problem will only increase unless solutions are found in time. One recent study, for example, predicted that America's growing population may generate 300 million tons (272 million metric tons) of trash by 2030. The amount of garbage produced also varies with the state of the economy; if times are good, people will buy more goods and produce more garbage. For example, many experts predict that population growth combined with rapid economic development in places such as China and India will create billions of new consumers and greatly add to the problem of worldwide waste.

1.5 MILLION TONS OF TRASH EACH DAY

"The real [garbage] problem is . . . [in] Asia. China, India, Indonesia, and Pakistan have a combined population of about 2.78 billion and discard over 1.5 million tons per day."—N.C. Vasuki, a former CEO of Delaware Solid Waste Authority.

N.C. Vasuki, "The Real World of Garbage," *MSW Management*, September–October 2004. www.mswmanagement.com/september-october-2004/real-world-garbage.aspx.

On the other hand, there are a few signs of hope for reducing the waste stream and addressing waste problems. For example, no one could have predicted the rise of recycling and yard waste composting over the last few decades, and more intensive recycling and waste strategies are already leading the way to keeping even greater volumes of trash out of landfills. And thanks to environmental advocacy by scientists, interest groups, and some

Garbage in Outer Space

Over the past few decades, humans have been spreading their garbage even into outer space. According to reports, between 9,000 and 15,000 pieces of debris can now be found orbiting the earth. The space garbage comes from satellites and various space missions undertaken by the United States, Russia, France, Japan, India, the European Space Agency, and China. The debris ranges in size from tiny specks to discarded parts of rockets weighing as much as 10 tons (9 metric tons). The orbiting trash eventually falls toward the earth, where it is burned up in the planet's atmosphere, but it can take a very long time for this to happen. In the meantime, the trash simply circles the planet, often colliding and breaking into smaller and smaller pieces. Scientists have warned that we are approaching a point at which the space junk could endanger future space programs. Although the danger is less for peopled spaceflights to the International Space Station, since most of the debris is located at higher altitudes, the junk can pose a risk to commercial and research flights that need to fly through the debris field. Currently, there is no economically viable method for cleaning up the debris.

companies, a new awareness about the need for greener, more sustainable living is slowly permeating the world's consciousness. These new attitudes about the connection between humans and the environment, along with new waste management technologies in the future, could lead the way to a more positive future for garbage management.

New Waste Management Strategies for the Future

If the world population continues to grow and the world economy continues to expand, experts agree that more effective waste management strategies will be necessary to minimize adverse impacts on the environment and human health. Many waste management officials believe that managing the world's garbage will depend on new technologies to dispose of garbage properly, prevent it from harming the environment, and turn it into energy. Other commentators advocate the adoption of programs to encourage or force consumers to reduce their waste. Still others see the need for more radical solutions, such as overhauling the world economy to make it more sustainable. Many new waste management ideas are now being tested and may become standard and affordable options in the future.

Modern Landfill Solutions

Modern landfill technology is already a vast improvement over older landfills and open-air dumps of the past. In the United States, new landfills are better designed and built in safer locations in order to reduce dramatically or prevent seepage of noxious water or gases into the environment. Although environmentalists worry these safety systems may one day break down, tests by the EPA and others have so far shown them to be far superior to older landfill designs. As the National Solid Wastes Management Association notes:

Modern landfills generate significantly lower concentrations of NMOCs [nonmethane organic compounds] than older sites. . . .

[Also,] the potential risks to human health and the environment of gases from modern landfills is significantly less than older landfills because the devices used to combust [burn] the gas have destruction efficiencies of more than 99 percent for methane and greater than 98 percent for all other NMOCs. [And] releases of trace constituents contained in the leachate from modern landfills are practically eliminated because leachate is collected, removed, and treated. . . .

Research has shown that leachate treatment facilities at modern landfills are capable of removing 100 percent of the trace organics and over 85 percent of the heavy metals.[49]

A worker sprays disinfectant over a modern landfill site in China. Modern landfill systems are being created to help the environment by reducing the amount of harmful emissions.

Modern landfill systems are employed mostly by developed countries. These methods may spread around the globe in the future as developing nations improve their waste management policies and are able to afford the technology.

The waste industry foresees the development of additional landfill innovations in the future that will further protect the environment and human health. One of the most promising ideas is the bioreactor landfill, a system that adds liquids and/or air to the waste in landfills in order to accelerate the biodegradation process, stabilize the landfill waste, and better seal it off from the surrounding environment. There are two types of bioreactor landfills: aerobic, or using oxygen, in which water and air are circulated through the landfill, which increases normal composting-type decomposition of the organic material; and anaerobic, or oxygen free, in which decomposition is stimulated simply by adding and recirculating liquids.

BIOREACTOR DRAWBACKS

"The bioreactor, with all its hazardous potential, is . . . fostering a system reliant on ever greater levels of wasting, no matter the environmental toll."—Heather Rogers, journalist, author, and filmmaker.

Heather Rogers, "Titans of Trash," *Nation*, December 19, 2005, p. 22.

The goal of both methods is to speed up methane and leachate production that otherwise would occur many years into the future, so that it can be quickly removed or used to produce energy. According to the National Solid Wastes Management Association, research has shown that bioreactor landfills generate air and water emissions for only about seven to ten years compared to thirty years for a conventional landfill. Cleaning many of the toxins from landfills in this way, supporters claim, allows for quicker return of the landfill properties to productive uses such as parks.

Another idea to reduce air emissions at landfills is the use of biocovers or "phytocapping"—basically using composted yard waste, living trees, or other vegetation to cover the waste. This creates a biologically active, natural filter that helps to oxidize and destroy methane emissions and other organic compounds as they seep from the ground, keeping them from polluting the environment. Living vegetation can also intercept rainfall, helping to prevent water from penetrating underlying landfill materials.

However, because of the possibility that all landfills will eventually leak their contents into the surrounding environment, landfill critics question the use of any type of landfill system in future waste management schemes. As the Grassroots Recycling Network puts it: "Landfills remain an antiquated and unsustainable method of resource management, a threat to public and environmental health, and a substantial contributor to climate change. Bioreactor technology will not mitigate [resolve] these issues and is merely a stop-gap measure that fails to address the real issue of wasted resources in this country."[50]

New Incineration Techniques

In addition to landfills, another waste management method that has been improved by technological advances is incineration, or the burning of garbage. Incineration-based processes for waste disposal have long been a subject of intense debate because of the harmful pollutants that can be emitted into the air, land, and water. The biggest concern about incineration is that it can produce significant amounts of dioxin and furan—substances known to cause cancer and other serious health hazards. And although incineration of wastes can sometimes produce energy, in the absence of good technology and strict controls, this process can release more harmful emissions than burning coal, one of the most polluting fossil fuels. As Canadian environmentalist Peter Tabuns warns, "When you burn garbage, you're putting out 33 per cent more carbon dioxide than when you burn coal, and the United Nations environment program says that 60 per cent of the world's dioxins come from burning garbage."[51]

Unlike older incinerators, however, new state-of-the-art incinerators substantially reduce the amount of leftover toxins to tiny quantities measurable only in picograms—each only a millionth of a millionth of a gram. To accomplish this feat, high-tech incinerators burn wastes at very high temperatures—between

An incineration plant in Tokyo, Japan, is shown here. Advanced technology has helped with incineration-based processes by reducing the amount of toxins and turning them into harmless solids.

1,832°F and 2,192°F (1,000°C and 1,200°C)—to reduce their toxic chemical components to harmless solids that can be used for road building or similar projects. In addition, technologies such as combustion chambers, rotation washers, condensation filters, and enormous catalytic converters are often used to remove toxins from gases created from the incineration process. This system, according to supporters, provides an efficient and green way to dispose of massive amounts of human waste.

INCINERATION STILL SAFE AND EFFECTIVE

"High temperature incineration will continue to play an important role in the future for the safe and effective treatment of the organic hazardous wastes that will continue to be generated by U.S. industry."—Environmental Technology Council, a trade association of commercial environmental firms.

Environmental Technology Council, "Hazardous Waste Incineration: Advanced Technology to Protect the Environment," February 2007. www.etc.org.

Modern, low-polluting incinerators are already a key strategy for some countries. Germany, for example, has become the leader in waste incineration technology, and the country is using this technology to incinerate highly hazardous wastes shipped from around the world. As reporters Udo Ludwig and Barbara Schmid relate: "Germany has become one of the major importers of hazardous waste from all over the planet, a giant waste disposal facility for the rest of the world. Munitions waste from Sweden, pesticides from Colombia, asbestos-contaminated rubble from the United States, solvents from China and lead-acid batteries from Montenegro."[52] German environmental ministers see their mission as part of the country's environmental responsibility, because otherwise many hazardous wastes would be improperly disposed of or dumped into the oceans. But Germany hopes that other countries will eventually build their own incinerators, using German technology. This may already be happening; China has plans to build two hazardous waste facilities using the German system.

Garbage to Energy Technologies

Wastes can also be used to generate clean energy, according to many experts. One method involves burning methane produced by landfills as a fuel source. The EPA reports that about four hundred landfills in the United States have methane power plants that can capture the methane produced by the landfill and turn it into electricity. In addition, garbage itself can create energy when it is burned. So-called waste-to-energy (WTE) plants incinerate municipal wastes to produce two important benefits—reducing the mass and weight of garbage by turning it into ash, and creating renewable electricity.

GARBAGE IS GOLD

"We now have the technology to take garbage, turn it into hydrogen gas, and feed it to a fuel cell to create clean electricity and heat, with virtually no emissions, no greenhouse gases released, and no combustion, period. Garbage to gold, pure and simple."—Fred Schwartz, vice president of Intellergy, a California energy company.

Fred Schwartz, "There's Power in All That Garbage," *Globe and Mail*, June 16, 2005, p. A21.

The WTE systems work by burning rubbish and using the heat to make steam, which drives a turbine and can generate electricity. In the United States, WTE plants are already a significant source of energy. As Diane Gow McDilda, a writer for *MSW Management*, explains:

> The Integrated Waste Services Association reports that today there are 89 WTE plants in operation in the US. Together they have the capacity to generate nearly 2,700 MW of electricity. This renewable form of energy production operates 24 hours a day, seven days a week, over 365 days a year to produce 17 billion kWh (kilowatt-hours, a measurement used by electric companies to

charge for electricity) of electricity. That's enough electricity to run 2.3 million homes in the US. WTE facilities account for nearly 20% of all renewable resource energy generation here in the [United States].[53]

Perhaps the most exciting type of garbage-to-energy technology, however, is plasma gasification, a process that reduces wastes to their harmless molecular components. As Joseph Longo, the founder of industry leader Startech Environmental Corporation, explains: "What's so devilishly wonderful about plasma gasification is that it's completely circular. . . . It takes everything back to its fundamental components in a way that's beautiful."[54] Writer Michael Behar explains how plasma technology works:

A 650-volt current passing between two electrodes rips electrons from the air, converting the gas into plasma. Current flows continuously through this newly formed plasma, creating a field of extremely intense energy very much like lightning. The radiant energy of the plasma arc is so powerful, it disintegrates trash into its constituent elements by tearing apart molecular bonds. The system is capable of breaking down pretty much anything except nuclear waste, the isotopes of which are indestructible. The only by-products are an obsidian-like glass used as a raw material for numerous applications, including bathroom tiles and high-strength asphalt, and a synthesis gas, or "syngas"—a mixture of primarily hydrogen and carbon monoxide that can be converted into a variety of marketable fuels, including ethanol, natural gas and hydrogen.[55]

Supporters believe that plasma plants will eventually replace landfills by providing a cheaper way to dispose of trash. Although a plasma converter plant would be expensive to build initially—roughly about $250 million—in large cities it could potentially pay for itself in ten or twenty years by eliminating the costs of landfill dumping and maintenance fees. After that, cities might even be able to make money with the plasma machines by selling the electricity, syngas, and glass that the plasma process produces.

"Waste to energy" incineration plants turn garbage into ash, which reduces its mass and weight, and creates renewable electricity. This power plant runs on burning household waste.

Plasma technology, however, is still unproven on a large scale and has attracted some critics. Brad Van Guilder, a scientist at the Ecology Center in Ann Arbor, Michigan, for example, says: "That obsidian-like slag contains toxic heavy metals and breaks down when exposed to water. . . . Dump it in a landfill, and it could one day contaminate local groundwater."[56] Other commentators worry about the environmental effects of syngas. As Monica Wilson, the international coordinator for the Global Alliance for Incinerator Alternatives, warns, "In the cool-down phases, the components in the syngas could re-form into toxins."[57]

Garbage Reduction Programs

Innovative trash collection systems may provide a different way to manage future garbage problems. One idea pioneered in some countries is "Pay-As-You-Throw," or PAYT—a type of garbage collection

One new type of garbage collection is "Pay-As-You-Throw," which charges customers based on the amount of trash that they generate. A man counts some of the new Wheelie bins that are being used in England as part of the "Pay-As-You-Throw" program.

that charges residents for the collection of municipal wastes based on the amount of trash they generate. Supporters of these programs argue that they create a financial incentive that helps to motivate consumers to recycle and reduce their trash. As the EPA explains: "Traditionally, residents pay for waste collection through property taxes or a fixed fee, regardless of how much—or how little—trash they generate. Pay-As-You-Throw (PAYT) breaks with tradition by treating trash services just like electricity, gas, and other utilities. Households pay a variable rate depending on the amount of service they use."[58]

Some PAYT programs bill customers based on the weight of their trash, while others charge by volume. Either way, the system has a proven record for reducing the volume of trash people throw away. As Matt Kallman of the environmental group World Resources Institute describes:

> Residents of the city of Maastricht [in the Netherlands] . . . must buy plastic garbage bags based on how much waste they expect to generate; larger bags cost more money. Since the introduction of the program, the city's recycling rate has increased from 45 percent to 65 percent. Other cities have similar programs based on weight, which is tracked by a computer chip embedded in trashcans; households are charged for the total amount of non-recyclable waste they produce.[59]

Japan also has had great success using PAYT. During the 1990s the country experienced a rising tide of trash due largely to excessive packaging used by Japanese manufacturers. As the United Nations Economic and Social Commission for Asia and the Pacific explains:

> Packaging offered by Japanese shops is unparalleled in other nations. For example, it is not unusual to find gift cartons of biscuits individually wrapped inside their boxes, nestled in corrugated papers inside a plastic bag in a tin or box, covered with wrapping paper and presented in a shopping bag. Basic grocery items like fruits, even single carrots, often come individually wrapped in cellophane.[60]

To fight this problem, many cities in Japan adopted PAYT programs, including the country's capital, Kyoto. As an article from the Web site Japan for Sustainability explains:

> Nine months after a new fee-based waste collection program was introduced in the city of Kyoto, the weight of household garbage generated by residents had dropped by 16.5 percent and the weight of recyclables was some 21 percent lower compared to the previous year, according to a city report released in November 2007. Over 50 percent of people that responded to a public survey on the new program, conducted by the city in February 2007, said that they had definitely changed their waste handling habits as a result.[61]

PAYT is now increasingly being adopted in thousands of cities in the United States. A 2006 EPA report found that nearly seventy-one hundred PAYT programs are operating in American cities, including thirty of the country's largest cities. The states of Minnesota, New Hampshire, Oregon, Washington, and Wisconsin have the most PAYT programs, and many other places are adopting PAYT programs at a rapid rate. The EPA estimates that the PAYT systems already reduce U.S. municipal solid wastes by 4.6 million to 8.3 million tons (4.2 million to 7.5 million metric tons) each year.

Kyoto Mechanisms

In developing countries, a program called Clean Development Mechanisms (CDM)—a creation of the 1997 Kyoto Protocol treaty on climate change—may help reduce methane emissions from garbage. The Kyoto Protocol is an amendment to the United Nations Framework Convention on Climate Change, an international treaty that seeks to reduce global warming by requiring industrialized countries to reduce the greenhouse gas emissions believed to be causing rising global temperatures. Using the treaty's CDM program, industrialized countries can claim credits for reducing global warming not only by reducing their own greenhouse gas emissions but also by funding greenhouse gas-reduction programs in less-developed nations. Methane, along

Solving the Problem of Plastic Bags

Plastic bags have become a ubiquitous convenience item in the modern world, used as shopping bags for groceries and every other type of product. They are strong, lightweight, and inexpensive. But plastic bags are also fast becoming one of the world's most widespread trash problems. According to the U.S. Environmental Protection Agency (EPA), the United States generates about 380 billion plastic bags a year and recycles less than 5 percent of them. Worldwide, only about 1 percent are recycled. When bags are not recycled or disposed of properly, they blow onto streets, flow into storm drains, or get caught up in trees, creating ugly litter. The bags also pollute rivers, lakes, and oceans. According to some environmental groups, when the bags are washed out to sea, marine animals such as sea turtles can mistake them for food and die after eating the plastic. They say other sea creatures get tangled in the bags and die. Makers of the plastic bags are trying to make recycling the bags easier for consumers and to use more recycled content in the bags they produce. Meanwhile, environmental groups encourage consumers to substitute reusable shopping bags for plastic bags and to think carefully about whether they even need a bag for smaller items.

Many plastic bags wash up on beaches or are washed out to sea, creating a huge trash problem if they are not disposed of properly.

The Clean Development Mechanisms (CDM) program allows countries to claim credits by reducing greenhouse gas emissions and by funding reduction programs in less-developed nations. Many CDM projects have been developed in China, like these cooling towers at an electrical power plant in Beijing.

with carbon, is one of the most dangerous greenhouse gases, and it is produced in large quantities by many of the developing world's open-air dumps. Because climate change is a global phenomenon, removing methane anywhere on the globe will help in the effort to reduce global warming. Some CDM projects focus on flaring methane caught at garbage dumps, while others aim to use the methane as fuel to create electricity.

A number of countries in Latin America became the first to seek CDM funding to establish methane-reduction systems, with Brazil the undisputed leader. Over three thousand CDM projects have been proposed in the region, and they are attracting investment capital in the range of $250 to $500 million. In recent years, however, the majority of CDM projects have been developed in India and China, due to their overwhelming problems with pollution Many observers think this is only the beginning, however. A new Kyoto treaty is expected to be negotiated for the period beginning in 2013, and these types of emissions-reducing programs could rise substantially in future years.

The United States signed the Kyoto Treaty, but U.S. president George W. Bush withdrew U.S. support for it and never submitted it for ratification by Congress. But the next U.S. president, Barack Obama, expressed support for the Kyoto process, so most observers expect the United States to reverse course and become very involved with the next Kyoto agreement and future global warming initiatives.

Zero Waste

The most far-reaching proposals for managing human garbage in the future involve the idea of "zero waste." Some proponents define this concept as simply a vast increase in the current model of consumer recycling of various types of wastes. Most zero waste advocates, however, say it requires instead a major restructuring of our manufacturing system to require producers to recycle 100 percent of their products and reuse the materials to create new products. As the Zero Waste Institute explains: "Zero waste states that the best way to avoid waste is to reuse everything over and over—perpetually. And that this can only be done if reuse is designed into all products, right from the start."[62]

Indeed, some commentators have said that the idea behind zero waste is to eliminate the very idea of waste. As writer Marc Gunther puts it: "Zero waste is just what it sounds like—producing, consuming, and recycling products without throwing anything away. Getting to a wasteless world will require nothing less than a total makeover of the global economy, which thinkers such as entrepreneur Paul Hawken, consultant Amory Lovins, and architect William McDonough have called the Next Industrial Revolution."[63]

No Escaping Hazardous Waste

"Large amounts of hazardous wastes will continue to be generated in the future even under optimistic but realistic expectations."—Environmental Technology Council, a trade association of commercial environmental firms.

Environmental Technology Council, "Hazardous Waste Incineration: Advanced Technology to Protect the Environment," February 2007. www.etc.org.

Architect and industrial designer William McDonough, for example, has been setting forth his ideas on zero waste since the early 1990s. McDonough envisions a world where factories produce completely safe products that require no regulation and can be easily remade into new goods. McDonough quite literally views this as the next phase for the world, the step that must follow the pollution-producing Industrial Revolution. As McDonough explains:

> The Industrial Revolution as a whole was not designed. It took shape gradually as industrialists and engineers figured out how to make things. The result is that we put billions of pounds of toxic materials in the air, water and soil every year and generate gigantic amounts of waste. If our goal is to destroy the world—to produce global warming and toxicity and endocrine disruption—we're doing great. But if the goal isn't global warming, what is? I want to crank the wheel of industry in a different direc-

tion to produce a world of abundance and good design— a delightful, safe world that our children can play in.[64]

McDonough would make this dream happen by convincing manufacturers to use sustainable "cradle-to-cradle" design, in which everything used to make products is either returned to the soil as nontoxic biodegradable nutrients or returned to industry, where it can be infinitely recycled into new products. Companies could accomplish this by employing new product designs that use only chemicals and materials that are completely safe— that is, by making major changes at the very beginning of the design and production process. As an example, McDonough has already helped design completely safe fabrics that use and produce absolutely no toxins in the manufacturing process. He is currently working with Fortune 500 companies and the government of China to transform many of his other ideas into reality.

Landfill Mining

One day waste experts say that humans may begin mining landfills for all the reusable materials dumped there over the last century. Since only about a third of all municipal garbage in the United States is recycled, landfills may be abundant sources of all kinds of recyclable materials —everything from plastics to aluminum cans to precious metals in old computers and other e-waste. The basic technology for such an effort is pretty simple: Screens are used to separate the soil from the waste, the remaining wastes are shredded into small pieces, and then magnets are used to pull out ferrous metals (metals that contain iron). Recently, this process has been developed even further, and now magnets are spun quickly, creating a current with an electrical effect that makes aluminum and other nonferrous metals levitate from other wastes. So far the mining idea has not taken off because it is still less costly to produce metals from mining ore than to extract them from landfills. The economics of landfill mining may soon change, however, as the developing world demands more of the world's resources and the price of metals such as aluminum, gold, and copper rise. Experts say it might only be a question of time before recycling expands to scour for treasures once buried as trash.

Whether the world can actually implement some of the various new strategies for managing wastes or ever reach McDonough's fantastic vision of a nontoxic world will be answered in coming decades, and possibly only by future generations. For now, these exciting technologies, programs, and ideas at least show what might be possible and provide humans with reasons to hope for a cleaner, safer future.

NOTES

Chapter 1: Garbage—Yesterday and Today

1. Susan Strasser, *Waste and Want: A Social History of Trash*. New York: Metropolitan, 1999, p. 12.
2. Strasser, *Waste and Want: A Social History of Trash*, p. 13.
3. Quoted in Joshua Jelly-Schapiro, "Talking Trash," *American Prospect*, December 28, 2005. www.prospect.org/cs/articles?article=talking_trash.
4. Blue Egg, "Landfills: Waste Is a Terrible Thing to Mind." www.blueegg.com/article/Landfills Waste-Is-a-Terrible-Thing-to-Mind.html.
5. Zero Waste America, "'BUYER BEWARE' . . . of Old Landfills and Contaminated Property!" www.zerowasteamerica.org/BuyerBeware.htm.
6. Natural Resources Defense Council, "Too Good to Throw Away: Recycling's Proven Record," February 1997. www.nrdc.org/cities/recycling/recyc/recyinx.asp.
7. Environmental Defense Fund, "Landfill Gas Capture: Cutting Emissions and Saving Money," April 18, 2008. http://m.edf.org/article.cfm?contentID=7816.
8. Environmental Defense Fund, "Environmental Defense Fund Takes Legal Action to Address Landfill Methane Emissions," Common Dreams.org, October 23, 2008. www.commondreams.org/newswire/2008/10/23-16.
9. Natural Resources Defense Council, "Too Good to Throw Away."
10. National Solid Wastes Management Association, "Modern Landfills: A Far Cry from the Past," August 2008. www.environmentalistseveryday.org/docs/research-bulletin-2008/Research-Bulletin-Modern-Landfill.pdf.
11. Daniel Benjamin, "The Eight Myths of Recycling," *American Enterprise*, January–February 2004.

12. Environmental Protection Agency, "Organobromine Production Wastes; Identification and Listing of Hazardous Waste; Land Disposal Restrictions; Listing of CERCLA Hazardous Substances, Reportable Quantities; Final Rule," *Federal Register*, May 4, 1998. www.epa.gov/osw/laws-regs/state/revision/frs/fr165.pdf.

Chapter 2: The Recycling Solution

13. Heather Rogers and Christian Parenti, "The Hidden Life of Garbage: Why Our Waste Keeps Growing," *Utne Reader*. www.utne.com/2002-11-01/The-Hidden-Life-of-Garbage.aspx.
14. Natural Resources Defense Council, "The Past, Present and Future of Recycling: Recycling's Up, but So Is Trash." www.nrdc.org/cities/recycling/fover.asp.
15. Quoted in Jacoba Charles, "San Francisco Closes the Lid on Garbage: Recycling and Composting Expected to Be Mandatory by Year's End," Mother Nature Network, April 15, 2009. www.plentymag.com/features/2008/06/recyling_san_francisco.php.
16. National Recycling Coalition, "Recycling Benefits: The Many Reasons Why." www.recycling-revolution.com/recycling-benefits.html.
17. National Recycling Coalition, "Recycling Benefits."
18. Helen Spiegelman, "Beyond Recycling: The Future of Waste," Grassroots Recycling Effort. www.grrn.org/zerowaste/articles/enough_spring_2003.html.
19. Quoted in Jelly-Schapiro, "Talking Trash."
20. Environmental Protection Agency, "Plastics." www.epa.gov/epawaste/conserve/materials/plastics.htm#recycle.
21. Emily Gurnon, "The Problem with Plastics: Recycling It Overseas Poses Risks to Workers. Doing It Here Doesn't Pay," Mindfully.org, June 5, 2003. www.mindfully.org/Plastic/Recycling/Problem-With-Plastics5jun03.htm.
22. Benjamin, "The Eight Myths of Recycling."
23. Benjamin, "The Eight Myths of Recycling."
24. Quoted in Jelly-Schapiro, "Talking Trash."
25. Rogers and Parenti, "The Hidden Life of Garbage."
26. Natural Resources Defense Council, "The Past, Present and Future of Recycling."

27. Spiegelman, "Beyond Recycling."

Chapter 3: Dealing with Hazardous Waste

28. Environmental Protection Agency, "Wastes—Hazardous Waste." www.epa.gov/osw/hazard/index.htm.

29. Environmental Protection Agency, "Guide for Industrial Waste Management." www.epa.gov/epawaste/nonhaz/indus trial/guide/index.htm.

30. Patty Martin, "Safe Food and Fertilizer: Food Is a Four-Letter Word," Article Archives, March 22, 2008. www.articlear chives.com/environment-natural-resources/toxic-hazardous -substances/885046-1.html.

31. Ezra Gold, "Nuclear Waste Disposal," University of Rochester. www.history.rochester.edu/class/EZRA/index.htm.

32. Paragon Green, "Toxic Trail: The E-Waste Problem," 2008–2009. www.tvtakeback.com/ewaste.html.

33. Environmental Protection Agency, "Wastes—Resources Conservation—Common Wastes & Materials—eCycling—Frequently Asked Questions," www.epa.gov/osw/conserve/materials/ecycling/faq.htm.

34. Green Health Live, "Electronics Make Lousy Landfill," May 23, 2008. www.greenhealthlive.com/index.php?main_page=document_general_info&products_id=205.

Chapter 4: Waste Management—A Global Challenge

35. Quoted in Elisabeth Rosenthal, "All of Europe Getting a Whiff of Naples Garbage Problem," *International Herald-Tribune*, June 8, 2008. www.iht.com/articles/2008/06/08/europe/trash.php.

36. Andreas Tzortzis, "Berlin: Sorting Trash with Conviction," *International Herald-Tribune*, February 21, 2007. www.iht.com/articles/2007/02/21/news/trashberlin.php.

37. Fabric of Nature, "Garbage and Landfills: Environmental Problems with Landfills." www.fabric-of-nature.com/prob lems-with-land-and-fresh-water/garbage-and-landfills.html.

38. Hisashi Ogawa, "Sustainable Solid Waste Management in Developing Countries," Global Development Research Center. www.gdrc.org/uem/waste/swm-fogawa1.htm.

39. World Bank, "Waste Management in China: Issues and Recommendations, Executive Summary," May 2005. http://

web.worldbank.org/WBSITE/EXTERNAL/COUNTRIES/EAS
TASIAPACIFICEXT/EXTEAPREGTOPURBDEV/0,,content
MDK:20535612~pagePK:34004173~piPK:34003707~the
SitePK:573913,00.html.

40. David Stanway, "China Bans Plastic Bags in Fight Against Pollution," *Guardian*, January 9, 2008. www.guardian.co.uk/
world/2008/jan/09/china.plasticbags.

41. Quoted in Anneli Rufus and Kristan Lawson, "Exporting
Garbage," *Plenty*, May 6, 2008. www.plentymag.com/ask/
2008/05/q_i_have_heard_that.php.

42. Quoted in Oliver Harvey, "Hidden Face of Olympic Hosts,"
Sun, August 5, 2008. www.thesun.co.uk/sol/homepage/news
/article1513560.ece#OTC-RSS&ATTR=News.

43. Harvey, "Hidden Face of Olympic Hosts."

44. Sebastian Knauer, Thilo Thielke, and Gerald Traufetter, "Profits for Europe, Industrial Slop for Africa," *Spiegel Online International*, September 18, 2006. www.spiegel.de/inter
national/spiegel/0,1518,437842,00.html.

45. Elizabeth Grossman, *High Tech Trash: Digital Devices, Hidden Toxics, and Human Health*. Washington, DC: Island, 2006, p. 5.

46. Justin Berton, "Continent-Size Toxic Stew of Plastic Trash
Fouling Swath of Pacific Ocean," *SF Gate*, October 19, 2007.
www.sfgate.com/cgi-bin/article.cgi?f=/c/a/2007/10/
19/SS6JS8RH0.DTL&hw=pacific+patch&sn=001&sc=1000.

47. Quoted in Berton, "Continent-Size Toxic Stew of Plastic Trash
Fouling Swath of Pacific Ocean."

48. Algalita Marine Research Foundation, "Plastic Debris from
Rivers to Sea." www.algalita.org/pdf/PLASTIC%20DEBRIS
%20ENGLISH.pdf.

Chapter 5: New Waste Management Strategies for the Future

49. National Solid Wastes Management Association, "Modern
Landfills."

50. Grassroots Recycling Network, "Garbage Is Not Renewable
Energy." www.grrn.org/landfill/notrenewableenergy/bioreac
tor.html.

51. Quoted in Canadian Press, "McGuinty Pushes Incineration,"

Star, March 28, 2007. www.thestar.com/News/article/19 6913.

52. Udo Ludwig and Barbara Schmid, "Germany's Booming Incineration Industry: Burning the World's Waste," *Spiegel Online International*, February 21, 2007. www.spiegel.de/international/spiegel/0,1518,467239,00.html.

53. Diane Gow McDilda, "The Power of Garbage: Waste-to-Energy Plants Are Eating It Up," *MSW Management*, October 2008. www.mswmanagement.com/october-2008/wte-waste-power.aspx.

54. Quoted in Michael Behar, "The Prophet of Garbage," *Popular Science*, March 1, 2007. www.popsci.com/scitech/article/2007-03/prophet-garbage.

55. Behar, "The Prophet of Garbage."

56. Quoted in Behar, "The Prophet of Garbage."

57. Quoted in Behar, "The Prophet of Garbage."

58. Environmental Protection Agency, "Pay-As-You-Throw." www.epa.gov/epawaste/conserve/tools/payt/index.htm.

59. Matt Kallman, "Talking Trash: The World's Waste Management Problem," World Resources Institute, June 18, 2008. http://earthtrends.wri.org/updates/node/314.

60. U.N. Economic and Social Commission for Asia and the Pacific, "Japan's Garbage Collection Fee." www.unescap.org/drpad/vc/conference/bg_jp_14_jgc.htm.

61. Japan for Sustainability, "Pay-As-You-Throw Program Reduces Household Waste in Kyoto," December 7, 2007. www.japanfs.org/en/pages/026871.html.

62. Zero Waste Institute, "Zero Waste Is a Third Generation Principle." www.zerowasteinstitute.org.

63. Marc Gunther, "The End of Garbage," *Fortune*, March 14, 2007. http://money.cnn.com/magazines/fortune/fortune_archive/2007/03/19/8402369/index.htm.

64. Quoted in Anne Underwood, "Designing the Future: In a New Interview Series, *Newsweek* Talks to a Leading Ecological Architect Whose Goal Is Nothing Less than Eliminating Waste and Pollution," *Newsweek*, May 16, 2005. www.newsweek.com/id/52058.

Chapter 1: Garbage—Yesterday and Today

1. According to the author, what effect did the Industrial Revolution have on the production of human garbage?
2. How much garbage, or municipal solid waste (MSW), did Americans generate in 2007?
3. What precautions are taken in building modern landfills to minimize harm to the environment and human health?

Chapter 2: The Recycling Solution

1. How did regulation by the U.S. Environmental Protection Agency (EPA) help to encourage the growth of recycling in the United States, according to the author?
2. What percentage of U.S. MSW was recycled in 2007?
3. Describe some of the problems associated with plastic recycling.

Chapter 3: Dealing with Hazardous Waste

1. According to the book, what types of household products fall into the category of hazardous wastes?
2. What types of hazardous wastes are produced by farms and agricultural producers?
3. What is the fastest growing type of hazardous waste, according to the author?

Chapter 4: Waste Management—A Global Challenge

1. What types of policies has Germany implemented to achieve a 75 percent recycling rate?
2. What are some of the problems associated with the exporting of trash to the developing world, according to most experts?
3. What is the Great Pacific Garbage Patch, and how does it threaten the environment and human health?

Chapter 5: New Waste Management Strategies for the Future

1. How does bioreactor technology work, according to the book?
2. What is plasma gasification?
3. Explain the concept of *zero waste*.

ORGANIZATIONS TO CONTACT

Basel Action Network (BAN)
Basel Action Network Secretariat, c/o Earth Economics
122 S. Jackson St., Ste. 320
Seattle, WA 98104
phone: (206) 652-5555
fax: (206) 652-5750
e-mail: inform@ban.org
Web site: www.ban.org

The BAN is a program of Earth Economics, a charitable organization based in Seattle, Washington. The program is dedicated to confronting the global environmental injustice and economic inefficiency of toxic wastes, products, and technologies and their devastating impacts. The program actively promotes banning the global waste trade and developing green, toxic-free design of consumer products. The Web site is an invaluable one-stop source of information about the Basel Convention and the effort to stop the global trade in toxic wastes, with a library, links to other organizations, a photo gallery, and a country-by-country report card on implementation of the Basel treaty.

Electronics TakeBack Coalition
phone: (415) 206-9595
e-mail: info@etakeback.org
Web site: www.computertakeback.com

The Electronics TakeBack Coalition is an organization that seeks to pressure producers of computers and other electronic products to collect their products at the end of the product life cycle and recycle hazardous electronic components. This Web site is a great source for news and articles on the subject of e-waste.

Keep America Beautiful
1010 Washington Blvd.
Stamford, CT 06901
phone: (203) 323-8987
fax: (203) 325-9199
e-mail: info@kab.org
Web site: www.kab.org

Keep America Beautiful is a volunteer-based community action and education organization that encourages individuals to take greater responsibility for improving their community's environment through litter prevention, waste minimization, recycling, and beautification programs. The group's Web site contains helpful tips on recycling, as well as fact sheets and other publications

National Recycling Coalition (NRC)
805 Fifteenth St. NW, Ste. 425
Washington, DC 20005
phone: (202) 789-1430
fax: (202) 789-1431
e-mail: info@nrc-recycle.org
Web site: www.nrc-recycle.org

The NRC is a national, nonprofit advocacy group dedicated to the advancement and improvement of recycling, waste prevention, composting, and reuse in North America. Its objective is to eliminate waste and promote sustainable economies through advancing sound management practices for raw materials. The NRC Web site is an excellent source for current articles on recycling and other waste issues.

Natural Resources Defense Council (NRDC)
40 W. Twentieth St.
New York, NY 10011
phone: (212) 727-2700
fax: (212) 727-1773
Web site: www.nrdc.org

The NRDC is a well-known environmental action group with 1.2

million members and more than 350 lawyers, scientists, and other professionals. The NRDC works on a broad range of environmental issues, including curbing global warming, protecting the oceans, and stemming the tide of toxic chemicals in the products we buy, the air we breathe, the food we eat, and the water we drink. The NRDC Web site provides a wealth of information on various subjects, including a section on recycling, with links to publications such as "Recycling 101," "The Past, Present and Future of Recycling," and "What to Do About E-waste."

Safe Food and Fertilizer
c/o Earth Island Institute
617 H St. SW
Quincy, WA 98848
phone: (509) 787-4275
e-mail: info@safefoodandfertilizer.org
Web site: www.safefoodandfertilizer.org/id10.html

Safe Food and Fertilizer, a project of the Earth Island Institute, is a grassroots citizens' organization that advocates a ban on the use of hazardous and other industrial wastes in fertilizers, soil amendments, and animal feed. The project's Web site provides a history of the issue of using hazardous wastes in fertilizers and other products and includes links to various government documents to explain the legal loophole that allows this to happen.

U.S. Environmental Protection Agency (EPA)
Ariel Rios Bldg.
1200 Pennsylvania Ave. NW
Washington, DC 20460
phone: (202) 272-0167
Web site: www.epa.gov

The EPA is a government agency responsible for protecting human health and safeguarding the natural environment. It works to protect Americans from environmental health risks, enforce federal environmental regulations, and to advocate environmental protection in U.S. policy.

The Waste Policy Center
104 Dry Mill Rd. SW, Ste. 103
Leesburg, VA 20175
phone: (703) 777-9800
fax: (703) 777-3733
e-mail: info@winporter.com
Web site: www.winporter.com

The Waste Policy Center is an environmental consulting, policy, and communications organization based in Leesburg, Virginia. The center's Web site offers a number of helpful publications on environmental and related subjects. These include the vest-pocket booklets *Trash Facts* and *Biotech Facts*, as well as reports such as *Recycling in America* and a color diagram on global climate change.

Zero Waste America (ZWA)
c/o Lynn Landes
217 S. Jessup St.
Philadelphia, PA 19107
phone: (215) 629-3553
e-mail: lynnlandes@earthlink.net
Web site: www.zerowasteamerica.org

The ZWA is an Internet-based environmental research organization specializing in the field of zero waste. The organization also specializes in U.S. waste disposal issues, including the lack of a federal waste management plan and the regulatory enforcement of the Resource Conservation and Recovery Act. The ZWA Web site provides information on waste-related legislative, legal, technical, environmental, health, and consumer issues. The Web site is a wonderful source for many types of information on zero waste and recycling, including photos, statistics, issue summaries, links to government agencies and other organizations, and various publications.

Books

E Magazine, *Green Living*. New York: Plume, 2005.

Rose George, *The Big Necessity: The Unmentionable World of Human Waste and Why It Matters*. New York: Metropolitan, 2008.

Elizabeth Grossman, *High Tech Trash: Digital Devices, Hidden Toxics, and Human Health*. Washington, DC: Island, 2006.

Salah El Haggar, *Sustainable Industrial Design and Waste Management: Cradle-to-Cradle for Sustainable Development*. St. Louis, MO: Academic Press, 2007.

R.E. Hester and Roy M. Harrison, *Environmental and Health Impact of Solid Waste Management Activities*. London: Royal Society of Chemistry, 2003.

Daniel Imhoff, *Paper or Plastic: Searching for Solutions to an Overpackaged World*. San Francisco: Sierra Club, 2005.

Heather Rogers, *Gone Tomorrow: The Hidden Life of Garbage*. New York: New Press, 2005.

Elizabeth Royte, *Garbage Land: On the Secret Trail of Trash*. New York: Little, Brown, 2005.

John Scanlan, *On Garbage*. London: Reaktion, 2005.

Susan Strasser, *Waste and Want: A Social History of Trash*. New York: Metropolitan Books, 1999.

Periodicals

Sean Cooper, "Houston, We Have a Trash Problem, *Wired*, April 24, 2007.

Economist, "The Truth About Recycling," June 7, 2007. www.economist.com/search/displaystory.cfm?story_id=9249262.

Donovan Hohn, "Sea of Trash," *New York Times Magazine*, June 22, 2008. www.nytimes.com/2008/06/22/magazine/22Plastics-t.html?_r=2&oref=slogin.

Alex Hutchinson, "Recycling Myths: PM Debunks 5 Half Truths About Recycling," *Popular Mechanics*, November 10, 2008. www.popularmechanics.com/science/earth/4290631.html.

Joshua Jelly-Schapiro, "Talking Trash," *American Prospect*, December 28, 2005. www.prospect.org/cs/articles?article=talking_trash.

Pamplin Media Group, "Don't Encourage Hawaii to Send Its Trash: Other States Should First Follow Oregon's Model for Recycling," *Portland* (OR) *Tribune*, June 17, 2008. www.portlandtribune.com/opinion/story.php?story_id=121371098611896800.

Gerry Popplestone, "China: 'A Global Garbage Dump,'" *Now Public*, September 7, 2008. www.nowpublic.com/environment/china-global-garbage-dump.

Heather Rogers, "Titans of Trash," *Nation*, November 30, 2005. www.gonetomorrow.org/articles.html.

Anna Shaff, "Keep Big Brother Out of My Trash: We Don't Need Government to Regulate Everything," *Christian Science Monitor*, August 11, 2008. www.csmonitor.com/2008/0811/p09s01-coop.html.

Nina Shapiro, "In the Future, Your Recycling Will Be Monitored and Dumpsters Will Be Trashed; That Is, If Chris Martin Gets His Way," *Seattle Weekly*, September 25, 2007. www.seattleweekly.com/2007-09-26/news/in-the-future-your-recycling-will-be-monitored-and-dumpsters-will-be-trashed.php.

John Tierney, "Recycling Is Garbage," *New York Times*, June 30, 1996. www.nytimes.com/1996/06/30/magazine/recycling-is-garbage.html.

Anne Underwood and Daniel Stone, "Green, Greener, Greenest: Many Universities Are Finding New Ways to Live and Learn in an Effort to Be Environmentally Friendly," *Newsweek*, August 18, 2008. www.newsweek.com/id/154357.

Internet Sources

BBC News, "Recycling Around the World," June 25, 2005. http://news.bbc.co.uk/2/hi/europe/4620041.stm.

Daniel K. Benjamin, "Eight Great Myths of Recycling," Property and Environment Research Center, September 2003. www.perc.org/pdf/ps28.pdf.

Jack Chang, "Scorned Trash Pickers Become Global Environmental Force," McClatchy Newspapers, March 24, 2008. www.mcclatchydc.com/226/story/31468.html.

Francesca Lyman, "Our Bodies, Our Landfills? You Are What You Ate, Breathed, Drank and More," Mindfully.org, February 5, 2003. www.mindfully.org/Health/2003/You-Are-What-You-Eat5feb03.htm.

Web Sites

Chartwell Solid Waste Group (www.wasteinfo.com). A useful source for waste industry research and analysis, with links to a wealth of reports, statistics, and waste-related organizations and agencies.

Circle of Life (www.circleoflife.org/resources.php?PHPSESSID =355e49f4c4e9584f9d416e6bca00a5f2). A Web site created by forest activist Julia Butterfly Hill containing a collection of guides on how individuals can recycle and live more sustainably.

MSW Management: Elements 2009 (www.mswmanagement .com/issues/index.aspx). An issue of the *Journal for Municipal Solid Waste Professionals* focusing on topics such as the recycling revolution, landfills, and waste-to-energy technologies.

U.S. Environmental Protection Agency, Office of Solid Waste (www.epa.gov/osw). A federal government Web site dedicated to the issues of waste management and recycling.

INDEX

A

Agriculture, 49–51
Air Pollution Control Act (1955),
    17
Algalita Marine Research
    Foundation, 72
American Plastics Council, 34
Anderson, Gary Dean, 41
Atomic Energy Act (1954), 52

B

Bali (Indonesia), 67
Basel Convention on the Control of
    Transboundary Movements of
    Hazardous Wastes and Their
    Disposal, 69-70, 69–70
Behar, Michael, 82
Benjamin, Donald K., 25, 37, 38–39
Berton, Justin, 71
Bioreactor landfills, 77, 78
Bloomberg, Michael, 38
British Columbia, 40, 42
Bush, George W., 56, 89

C

Carson, Rachel, 28
Carter, Jimmy, 48
Center for Food Safety, 48
Chabot, Warner, 71
Chemicals
    in municipal garbage, 21–22
    See also Hazardous waste
China
    solid waste generation and, 66
    trash imports to, 66, 68

Chlorofluorocarbons (CFCs), 46
Choi, Jamie, 68
Clean Development Mechanisms
    (CDM), 86, 89
Composting, 33
Comprehensive Environmental
    Response, Compensation, and
    Liability Act (CERCLA, 1980), 53
Côte d'Ivoire, dumping of toxic
    sludge in, 68 69

D

Deep well injection, 52, 52–53
Developing countries
    garbage situation in, 9, 63–66
    trash exports to, 66, 68
Dumps, public, 6–7
    See also Landfills

E

Earth Day, 29
Electronics TakeBack Coalition, 58–
    59
Energy
    benefits of recycling to, 35
    renewable, 81–82
Environment, 34–35
Environmental movement, birth of,
    28–29
Environmental Protection Agency
    (EPA), 6, 14
    on cancers, 23
    creation of, 17, 29
    on hazardous waste, 44
    on household hazardous waste, 46

on industrial hazardous waste, 49
inventory of Superfund sites by, 54
on landfill linings, 27
on recycling/composting, 31
rules on landfill operations, 18
on three R's of conservation, 32
on U.S. generation of plastic bags, 87
Environmental Technology Council, 90
Europe
  Green Dot system in, 43
  waste management in, 60–63
E-waste (consumer electronics), 9, 22, 57–59
  export to developing nations, 70–71
Extended Producer Responsibility (EPR), 40, 42

F
Fabric of Nature (Web site), 64
Fertilizers, 49–51
Fresh Kills landfill (Staten Island, NY), 6–7, 8

G
Garbage
  amount discarded by Americans, 6, 14
  history of, 11–14
  in outer space, 74
  reducing amount of, 35
Gattuso, Dana Joel, 59
Germany
  Green Dot system in, 41, 43
  recycling in, 62–63
Gold, Ezra, 56
Grassroots Recycling Network, 78
Great Pacific Garbage Patch, 71
Greece, garbage problem in, 61–62
Green Dot system (Germany), 41, 43

Greenpeace, 71–72
Grossman, Elizabeth, 70
Gunther, Marc, 90
Gurnon, Emily, 37–38, 63

H
Harvey, Oliver, 68
Hawken, Paul, 90
Hazardous waste
  agricultural, 49–51
  consumer electronics, 57–59
  examples of, 44
  export to developing nations, 68–70
  household products as, 44–46
  industrial, 46–49
  nuclear, 55–57
  recycling of, 32
  regulation of, 51–53
Heavy metals, 22
  in E-waste, 58–59
  in fertilizer, 50
Hooker Chemical Corporation, 47–48
Household products, 21, 44–46

I
Incinerators/incineration, 17, 79
  air pollution from, 25
  new techniques in, 78, 80
Industrial Revolution, 13, 90
Italy, 62

J
Junk dealers, 12–13

K
Kallman, Matt, 85
Kyoto Protocol (1997), 86, 89

L
Landfills, 7
  bioreactor, 77, 78

capacity of, 26–27
decline in number of, 19
EPA regulation of, 18
health dangers to people living near, 22–24
health/environmental improvements in, 25
leachate from, 21
as major source of methane emissions, 24
mining of, 91
reduction of gases from, 75–76, 77–78
safeguards in, 8–9
Leachate, 20, 21
deterioration of collection systems for, 27
EPA requirement to collect, 18
Lead, 22, 59
Lomborg, Bjorn, 20, 38
Longo, Joseph, 82
Love Canal (NY), 47, 47–49
Lovins, Amory, 90

M
Manila (Philippines), garbage dumps in, 65
Mann, Nick, 62
Martin, Patty, 49–50
McDilda, Diane Gow, 81–82
McDonough, William, 90–91, 92
Medical Waste Tracking Act (1988), 52
Mercaptan, 69
Mercury, 22, 25, 52, 59
Methane, 86
as greenhouse gas, 24, 89
leakage from old municipal dumps, 21
release from landfills, 9
Mobro (garbage barge), 29, 29
Moore, Charles, 71
Municipal solid waste (MSW), 6

categories of, before recycling, 16
China as leading producer of, 66
components of, 14–15
tons produced, by year, 15

N
National Recycling Coalition, 34, 35
National Solid Waste Management Association, 75–76, 77
on health/environmental improvements in modern landfills, 25
Natural Resources Defense Council (NRDC), 20–21, 39
Newsom, Gavin, 32
Nixon, Richard, 17
Non-methane organic compounds (NMOCs), 76
Nuclear Waste Policy Act (1982), 56
Nuclear wastes, 55–57

O
Obama, Barack, 89
Ogawa, Hisashi, 65
Outer space, debris in, 74

P
Packaging, 36
programs to reduce use of, 43
Parenti, Christian, 30
Pay-As-You-Throw (PAYT), 83, 85
Perchloroethylene, 21
Pesticides, 21
Phthalate, 21
Plasma gasification, 82–83
Plastic bags, 87
moves to ban, 39–40
Plastic Debris in the World's Oceans (Greenpeace), 71–72
Plastics, 36
as pollutant of oceans, 71–73

problems in recycling of, 37–38
recyclable types of, 33–34
Pollution
    air, 24, 25
    of groundwater, 8, 25, 47, 49, 83
    of world oceans by plastic, 71–73
Probo Koala (Dutch tanker), 68–69,
    69
Prystay, Chris, 58

R
Recycling
    future of, 39–40, 42–43
    in Germany, 62–63
    in history, 11–13
    items in curbside programs, 32–33
    limits of, 35–39
    mechanization and decline in,
        13–14
    municipal programs for, 31–32
    of municipal solid waste, 15
    of plastics, 33–34
Recycling content symbol, 41
Resource Conservation and
    Recovery Act (1976), 17
Resource Conservation and
    Recovery Act (RCRA, 1976),
    51–52
Resource Recovery Act (1970), 17
Rogers, Heather, 14, 30, 36, 39, 77

S
San Francisco (CA), recycling
    program in, 32
Schwartz, Fred, 81
Seattle (WA), recycling program in,
    31–32
Sewage sludge, 50–51
Silent Spring (Carson), 28–29
Simon, Deanna, 32

Society of Plastics Industries, 33–34
Solid Waste Disposal Act (1965),
    17, 51
Spiegelman, Helen, 40, 42
Strasser, Susan, 11–12, 13, 40
Superfund sites, 53–55
    megasites, 53
Synthetic gas (syngas), 82, 83

T
Tabuns, Peter, 78
Tang Hou, 66
Toxic Substances Control Act
    (1976), 51
Trichloroethylene, 21
Tzortzis, Andreas, 63

U
United Kingdom, , 62
United States, 39
Uranium mining, 55, 57

V
Van Guilder, Brad, 83
Vasuki, N.C., 73

W
Waste management companies, 18–
    19
Waste-to-energy (WTE) plants, 81–
    82
Wilson, Monica, 83
World Bank, 66

Y
Yucca Mountain (NV), 56

Z
Zero Waste Institute, 89

PICTURE CREDITS

ABOUT THE AUTHOR

Debra A. Miller is a writer and lawyer with a passion for current events, history, and public policy. She began her law career in Washington, D.C., where she worked on legislative, policy, and legal matters in government, public interest, and private law firm positions. She now lives with her husband in Encinitas, California. She has written and edited numerous books and anthologies on historical, political, health, environmental, and other topics.